Fitness
and
Wellness

Werner W.K. Hoeger
Sharon A. Hoeger

Boise State University

MP

Morton Publishing Company

925 W. Kenyon Ave., Unit 12
Englewood, Colorado 80110

With infinite love to our parents and children.

The authors wish to thank all those individuals who so graciously donated their time and efforts to make this work possible. Charles B. Scheer for the cover photographs; Dr. Glenn Potter for his support and encouragement; and Rachel Banashek, Cherianne Calkins, Brian Crossland, and Anne Staker for their help with the photography in this book.

Copyright © 1990 by Morton Publishing Company

Printed in the United States of America

10 9 8 7 6 5 4 3 2 1

ISBN: 0-89582-208-3

Preface

More than ever before Americans realize that good health is largely self-controlled and that premature illness and mortality can be prevented through adequate fitness and positive lifestyle habits. The current American way of life, unfortunately, does not provide the human body with sufficient physical exercise to maintain adequate health. Furthermore, many present lifestyle patterns are such a serious threat to our health that they actually increase the deterioration rate of the human body and often lead to premature illness and mortality.

Recent scientific research clearly indicates that active people live longer and enjoy a better quality of life. As a result, the importance of sound fitness programs has taken an entire new dimension. From an initial fitness fad in the early 1970s, fitness programs have become a trend that is now very much a part of the American way of life.

Nevertheless, while people in the United States are firm believers in the benefits of physical activity and positive lifestyle habits as a means to promote better health, most do not reap these benefits because they do not know how to implement a good fitness program that will indeed yield the desired results. Therefore, the information presented in this book has been written with this purpose in mind: to provide you with the necessary guidelines to implement a lifetime exercise and healthy lifestyle program so you can make a constant and deliberate effort to stay healthy and realize your highest potential for well-being.

Preface

Contents

The Importance of Physical Fitness

1

During the last two decades there has been a tremendous increase in the number of people participating in physical fitness programs. From an initial fitness fad in the early 1970s, fitness programs have become a trend that is now very much a part of the American way of life. The increase in the number of fitness participants is attributed primarily to scientific evidence linking vigorous exercise and positive lifestyle habits to better health and improved quality of life.

Unfortunately, the current American way of life does not provide the human body with sufficient physical exercise to maintain adequate health. Furthermore, many present lifestyle patterns are such a serious threat to our health that they actually increase the deterioration rate of the human body and often lead to premature illness and mortality.

Although people in the United States are firm believers in the benefits of physical activity and positive lifestyle habits as a means to promote better health, most do not reap these benefits because they do not know how to implement a sound fitness program that will indeed yield the desired results. According to the U.S. Department of Health and Human services, less than half of the adult population in the United States exercises regularly and only 10 to 20 percent exercise vigorously enough to develop the cardiovascular system.

Patty Neavill is a typical example of someone who often tried to change her life around, but was unable to do so because she did not know how to implement a healthy-lifestyle program. At age 24, Patty, a college sophomore, was discouraged with her weight, level of fitness, self-image, and quality of life in general. She had struggled with her weight for most of her life. Like thousands of other people, she had made many unsuccessful attempts to lose weight. Patty put her fears aside and decided it was time to enroll in a fitness course. As part of the course requirement, a battery of fitness tests was administered at the beginning of the semester. Patty's cardiovascular fitness and strength ratings were poor, her flexibility classification was average, she weighed over 200 pounds, and her percent body fat was 41.

Following the initial fitness assessment, Patty met with her course instructor who prescribed an exercise and nutrition program such as is presented in this book. Patty fully committed to carry out the prescription. She walked or jogged five times per week, worked out with weights twice a week, and played volleyball or basketball two to four times per week. Her daily caloric intake was in the range of 1,500 to 1,700 calories. Care was taken to meet the minimum required servings from the four food groups each day, which contributed about 1,200 calories to her diet. The remainder of the calories came primarily from complex carbohydrates. At the end of the sixteen-week semester, Patty's cardiovascular fitness, strength, and flexibility ratings had all improved to the good category, she lost 50 pounds, and her percent body fat had decreased to 22.5!

A thank-you note from Patty to the course instructor at the end of the semester read:

> *"Thank you for making me a new person. I truly appreciate the time you spent with me. Without your kindness and motivation, I would have never made it. It is great to be fit and trim. I've never had this feeling before and I wish everyone could feel like this once in their life. Thank you, Your trim Patty!"*

Patty was never taught the principles for implementing a fitness program. The information presented in this book has been written with this purpose in mind: to provide the reader with the necessary guidelines to implement a healthy lifestyle program. In Patty's case, not only did she need to obtain this knowledge, but like most Americans who have never "experienced fitness," she needed to be in a structured exercise setting to truly feel the joy of being physically fit. It is precisely for this reason that fitness and wellness courses are being offered in colleges and universities throughout the country.

LIFESTYLE, HEALTH, AND QUALITY OF LIFE

Many research findings have shown that physical inactivity and negative lifestyle habits are a serious threat to an individual's health. Movement and activity are basic functions needed by the human organism to grow, develop, and maintain health. However, physical activity is no longer a natural part of our existence. We live in an automated world where most of the activities that used to require strenuous physical exertion can be accomplished by machines with the simple pull of a handle or push of a button. For instance, if there is a need to go to a store that may only be a couple of blocks away, most people drive their automobiles and then spend several minutes driving around the parking lot in an effort to find a spot ten yards closer to the store's entrance. The groceries do not even have to be carried out anymore. They are usually taken out in a cart and placed in the vehicle by a youngster working at the store.

Similarly, during a normal visit to a multi-level shopping mall, it can easily be observed that almost everyone chooses to ride the escalators instead of taking the stairs. Automobiles, elevators, escalators, telephones, intercoms, remote controls, electric garage door openers, etc., are all modern-day commodities that minimize the amount of movement and effort required by the human body.

One of the most significant detrimental effects of modern-day technology has been an increase in chronic conditions which are related to a lack of physical activity (e.g., hypertension, heart disease, chronic low back pain, and obesity). These conditions are also referred to as hypokinetic diseases. The term "hypo" implies low or little, and "kinetic" implies motion. While lack of vigorous physical activity is a fact of modern life that most people can no longer avoid, if we want to enjoy many of the twentieth-century commodities and still expect to live life to its fullest, a lifetime exercise program must become a part of daily living.

With the new developments in technology, three additional factors have significantly changed our lives and have had a negative effect on human health: nutrition, stress, and environment. Fatty foods, sweets, alcohol, tobacco use, excessive stress (distress), and pollution in general have detrimental effects on people.

As the incidence of chronic diseases increased, it became obvious that prevention was the best medicine when dealing with these new health problems. Estimates indicate that over 50 percent of all disease is self-controlled, 64 percent of the factors contributing to mortality are caused by lifestyle and environmental factors, and that 83 percent of all deaths in the United States prior to the age of sixty-five are preventable. Most Americans are threatened by the very lifestyles they lead today.

The leading causes of death in the country today are basically lifestyle related (see Table 1.1). About 70 percent of all deaths are caused by cardiovascular disease (includes heart disease and cerebro-vascular diseases) and cancer. Approximately 80 percent of these could be prevented through a positive lifestyle program. Accidents are the third cause

TABLE 1.1. Leading Causes of Death in the United States: 1987

Cause	Total Number of Deaths	Percent of Total Deaths
1. Major cardiovascular diseases	963,611	45.4
2. Cancer	476,927	22.5
3. Accidents	95,020	4.5
4. Chronic obstructive pulmonary disease	78,380	3.7
5. All other causes	509,385	24.0

Source: Advance Report of Final Mortality Statistics, 1987. National Center for Health Statistics, U.S. Department of Health and Human Services.

of death. While not all accidents are preventable, many are. A significant amount of fatal accidents are related to alcohol and lack of use of seat belts. The fourth cause of death, chronic obstructive pulmonary disease, is largely related to tobacco use.

PHYSICAL FITNESS

The American Medical Association defines fitness as the general capacity to adapt and respond favorably to physical effort. This implies that individuals are physically fit when they can meet ordinary as well as the unusual demands of daily life safely and effectively without being overly fatigued and still have energy left for leisure and recreational activities. Physical fitness can be classified into two categories: health-related fitness and motor skill-related fitness. Most authorities agree that from a health point of view, there are four components of physical fitness (see Figure 1.1). These components are:

- **Cardiovascular endurance** — the ability of the heart, lungs, and blood vessels to supply oxygen and nutrients to the muscles for sustained exercise.

- **Muscular strength and endurance** — the ability of the muscles to generate force.

- **Flexibility** — the capacity of a joint to move freely through a full range of motion.

- **Body composition** — the amount of lean body mass and adipose tissue (fat mass) found in the human body.

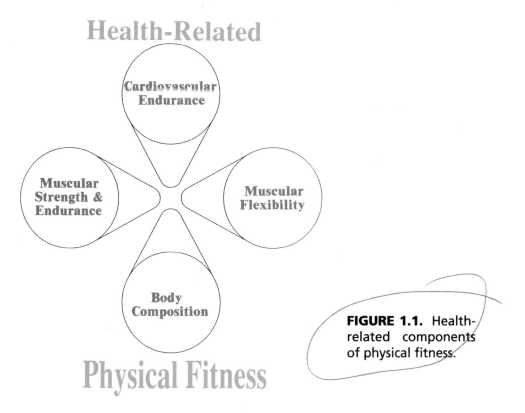

FIGURE 1.1. Health-related components of physical fitness.

To improve overall fitness, an individual has to participate in specific programs to develop each one of the four basic components. Nevertheless, after the initial fitness boom swept across the country in the 1970s, it became clear that just improving the four components of physical fitness alone would not always decrease the risk for disease and insure better health. As a result, a new concept developed in the 1980s that goes beyond the basic components of fitness. This new concept is referred to as "wellness", which can be defined as the constant and deliberate effort to stay healthy and achieve the highest potential for well-being.

The term wellness implies an all-inclusive umbrella composed of a variety of activities aimed at helping individuals recognize components of lifestyle that are detrimental to their health, and then implement principles and programs to change their behavior so as to improve the quality of life and achieve total well-being. This new concept goes far beyond absence of disease and optimal physical fitness. Wellness incorporates such aspects as adequate fitness, proper nutrition, spirituality, smoking cessation, stress management, substance abuse control, disease prevention and risk reduction, physical examinations, health education, and environmental support. Additional information on wellness and the implementation of a wellness program will be discussed in Chapter 5.

The motor skill-related aspects of fitness are of greater significance in athletics. In addition to the previous four components, motor skill-related fitness, as illustrated in Figure 1.2, includes agility, balance, coordination, power, reaction time, and speed. While these components are important in achieving success in athletics, they are not crucial for the development of better health. Therefore, in this book only the health-related components of fitness will be discussed.

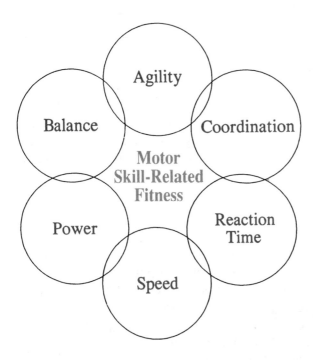

FIGURE 1.2.
Motor-Skill Components of Physical Fitness.

Benefits of Fitness Programs

Although many benefits can be enjoyed as a result of participating in a regular physical fitness program, the greatest benefit of all is that individuals enjoy a better quality of life. Even though there are some indications that they will also live a longer life, statistically this is difficult to prove because of the many different factors that can have an effect on our health and well-being. Several scientific research studies, nevertheless, are beginning to show an inverse relationship between exercise and premature mortality rates. However, when it comes to quality of life, there is no question that physically fit individuals who lead a positive lifestyle live a better and healthier life. These people can enjoy life to its fullest potential with a lot fewer health problems than inactive individuals who may also be indulging in negative lifestyle patterns. While it is difficult to compile an all-inclusive list of the benefits of physical fitness and wellness, the following list provides a summary of many of these benefits.

1. Improves and strengthens the cardiovascular system (improves oxygen supply to all parts of the body, including the heart, muscles, and the brain).
2. Improves muscular tone, muscular strength, and muscular endurance.
3. Improves muscular flexibility.
4. Helps maintain ideal body weight.
5. Improves posture and physical appearance.
6. Decreases the risk for chronic diseases and illnesses (heart disease, strokes, high blood pressure, pulmonary disease, arthritis etc.).
7. Relieves tension and helps in coping with stresses of life.
8. Increases levels of energy and job productivity.
9. Slows down the aging process.
10. Improves self-image and morale and aids in fighting depression.
11. Motivates toward positive lifestyle changes (better nutrition, smoking cessation, alcohol and drug abuse control).
12. Decreases recovery time following physical exertion.
13. Speeds up recovery following injury and/or disease.
14. Regulates and improves overall body functions.
15. Eases the process of childbearing and childbirth.
16. Improves the quality of life.

THE PATH TO FITNESS AND BETTER QUALITY OF LIFE

As a result of current scientific data and the fitness movement of the past two decades, most people in the country now see a need to participate in fitness programs to improve and maintain adequate health. Fitness needs, nevertheless, vary significantly from one person to the other. Consequently, exercise prescriptions should be individualized to obtain optimal results. The information presented in the next four chapters has been developed to provide you with the necessary information to write a lifetime program to improve physical fitness and to promote preventive health care and personal wellness. In the ensuing chapters you will learn how to:

- Determine whether medical clearance is required for safe exercise participation.

- Assess your overall level of physical fitness, including cardiovascular endurance, muscular strength and endurance, muscular flexibility, and body composition.

- Prescribe personal programs for total fitness development.

- Develop an adequate nutrition and weight control program.

- Implement a healthy-lifestyle program that includes prevention of cardiovascular diseases, cancer, stress management, and smoking cessation.

- Discern between myths and facts of exercise and health-related concepts.

GETTING STARTED

While exercise testing and/or participation is quite safe for most individuals, there is a small but real risk for exercise induced abnormalities in people with a history of cardiovascular problems and/or those who are at higher risk for disease. These people should be screened prior to initiating or increasing the intensity of an exercise program. Therefore, before you start an exercise program or participate in any exercise testing, fill out the questionnaire given in Figure 1.3. A positive answer to any of these questions may require a physician's approval prior to exercise participation. If there are no contraindications to exercise testing and/or participation, you can proceed to Chapter 2 to assess your current level of fitness.

EXERCISE CONSENT AND HEALTH HISTORY FORM

While exercise participation is relatively safe for most apparently healthy indi-viduals, the reaction of the cardiovascular system to increased levels of physical activity cannot always be totally predicted. Consequently, there is a small but real risk of certain changes occurring during exercise participation. Some of these changes may include abnormal blood pressure, irregular heart rhythm, fainting, and in rare instances a heart attack or cardiac arrest. It is imperative, therefore, that you provide honest answers to this questionnaire. Exercise may be contra-indicated under some of the conditions listed below, while others may simply require special consideration. **If any of the conditions apply, you should consult your physician before you participate in an exercise program.** You should also promptly report to your instructor any exercise-related abnormalities that you may experience during the course of the semester.

Have you ever had or do you now have any of the following conditions?

_____ 1.   Cardiovascular disease (any type of heart or blood vessel disease, including strokes)

_____ 2.   Elevated blood lipids (cholesterol and triglycerides)

_____ 3.   Chest pain at rest or during exertion

_____ 4.   Shortness of breath or other respiratory problems

_____ 5.   Uneven, irregular, or skipped heartbeats (including a racing or flutter-ing heart)

_____ 6.   Elevated blood pressure

_____ 7.   Diabetes

_____ 8.   Any joint, bone, or muscle problems (e.g., arthritis, low back pain, rheumatism, etc.)

_____ 9.   An eating disorder (anorexia, bulimia)

_____10.   Any other concern regarding your ability to safely participate in an exercise program? If so, explain: _____

_____

_____

Indicate if any of the following two conditions apply:

_____11.   Do you smoke cigarettes?

_____12.   Are you forty-five years or older?

Student's Signature: _____ Date: _____

FIGURE 1.3.

Physical Fitness Components and Assessment

2

The health-related components of physical fitness include cardiovascular endurance, muscular strength and endurance, muscular flexibility, and body composition. These four components will be discussed in this chapter along with basic techniques frequently used in their assessment. Using these assessment techniques, you will be able to regularly determine your physical fitness level as you engage in your exercise program. You are encouraged to take these tests at least twice. Once, as a pre-test, which will serve as a starting point to your exercise program; and later as a post-test, to assess improvements in fitness following ten to fourteen weeks of exercise participation.

The personal fitness profile in Figure A.1 (Appendix A) has been provided for you to record the results of each one of the fitness assessments in this chapter (pre-test). Figure A.2 can be used at the end of the term to record the results of your post-test. You may also obtain a computerized fitness profile by using the software for this book available to your instructor through Morton Publishing Company. An example of such a profile is shown in Figure A.3. In Chapter 3 you will also have the opportunity to write personal fitness goals for this course (see Figure 3.9). These goals should be based on the actual results of your initial fitness assessments. As you proceed with your exercise program, allow a minimum of eight weeks prior to your post-fitness assessments.

As has been discussed in Chapter 1, exercise testing and/or exercise participation is contraindicated for individuals with certain medical or physical conditions. Therefore, before you start an exercise program or participate in any exercise testing, be sure to fill out the exercise consent and health history form given in Figure 1.3. If your answer to any of the questions is positive, you should consult your doctor before initiating, continuing, or increasing your level of physical activity.

CARDIOVASCULAR ENDURANCE

Cardiovascular endurance, cardiovascular fitness, or aerobic fitness has been defined as the ability of the lungs, heart, and blood vessels to deliver adequate amounts of oxygen and nutrients to the cells to meet the demands of prolonged physical activity. As a person breathes, part of the oxygen contained in ambient air is taken up in the lungs and transported in the blood to the heart. The heart is then responsible for pumping the oxygenated blood through the circulatory system to all organs and tissues of the body. At the cellular level, oxygen is used to convert food substrates, primarily carbohydrates and fats, into energy necessary for physical activity, body functions, and to maintain a constant internal equilibrium.

Some examples of activities that promote cardiovascular or aerobic fitness are walking, jogging, cycling, rowing, swimming, cross-country skiing, aerobic dance, soccer, basketball, and racquetball. The necessary guidelines to develop a lifetime cardiovascular exercise program are given in Chapter 3.

A sound cardiovascular endurance program greatly contributes toward the enhancement and maintenance of good health. The "typical" American is not exactly a good role model when it comes to physical fitness. A poorly conditioned heart which has to pump more often just to keep a person alive is subject to more wear-and-tear than a well-conditioned heart. In situations where strenuous demands are placed on the heart, such as doing yard work, lifting heavy objects or weights, or running to catch a bus, the unconditioned heart may not be able to sustain the strain.

Every individual who initiates a cardiovascular exercise program can expect a number of benefits that result from training. Among these benefits are a decrease in resting heart rate, blood pressure, blood lipids (cholesterol and triglycerides), recovery time following exercise, and risk for hypokinetic diseases (those associated with physical inactivity and sedentary living). There is also an increase in cardiac muscle strength and oxygen-carrying capacity in the body.

Cardiovascular endurance is determined by the maximal amount of oxygen that the human body is able to utilize per minute of physical activity. This value is commonly expressed in milliliters of oxygen per kilogram of body weight per minute of physical activity (ml/kg/min). Since all tissues and organs of the body utilize oxygen to function, a higher amount of oxygen consumption indicates a more efficient cardiovascular system.

FIGURE 2.1. Aerobic activities promote cardiovascular development and help decrease the risk for chronic diseases.

During physical exertion, a greater amount of energy is needed to carry out the work. As a result, the heart, lungs, and blood vessels have to deliver more oxygen to the cells to supply the required energy to accomplish the task. During prolonged physical activity, an individual with a high level of cardiovascular endurance is able to deliver the required amount of oxygen to the tissues with relative ease. The cardiovascular system of a person with a low level of endurance would have to work much harder, since the heart would have to pump more often to supply the same amount of oxygen to the tissues, and consequently would fatigue faster. Hence, a higher capacity to deliver and utilize oxygen (oxygen uptake) indicates a more efficient cardiovascular system.

The 1.5-Mile Run Test

The most frequently used test to determine cardiovascular fitness is the 1.5-mile run test. Your fitness category is determined according to the time it takes to run/walk a 1.5-mile course. The only equipment necessary to conduct this test is a stopwatch and a track or premeasured 1.5-mile course.

The 1.5-mile run test is quite simple to administer, but caution should be taken when conducting the test. Since the objective of the test is to cover the distance in the shortest period of time, the use of this test should be limited to conditioned individuals who have been cleared for exercise. It is contraindicated for unconditioned beginners, symptomatic individuals, and those with known cardiovascular disease and/or heart disease risk factors. Unconditioned beginners are encouraged to have at least six weeks of aerobic training prior to taking this test.

Prior to taking the 1.5-mile run test you should conduct a few warm-up exercises. Do some stretching exercises, some walking, and slow jogging. Next, time yourself during the run/walk to see how fast you cover the distance. If any unusual symptoms arise during the test, do not continue. Stop immediately, see your physician and/or retake the test after another six weeks of aerobic training. At the end of the test, cool down by walking or jogging slowly for another three to five minutes. According to your performance time, look up your estimated maximal oxygen uptake in and your corresponding fitness category in

For example, a twenty-year-old female runs the 1.5-mile course in 12 minutes and 40 seconds. Table 2.1 shows a maximal oxygen uptake of 39.8 ml/kg/min for a time of 12:40. According to Table 2.2, this maximal oxygen uptake would place her in the good cardiovascular fitness category.

TABLE 2.1. Estimated Maximal Oxygen Uptake in ml/kg/min for the 1.5-mile Run Test.

Time	Max VO$_2$	Time	Max VO$_2$	Time	Max VO$_2$	Time	Max VO$_2$
6:10	80.0	9:30	54.7	12:50	39.2	16:10	30.5
6:20	79.0	9:40	53.5	13:00	38.6	16:20	30.2
6:30	77.9	9:50	52.3	13:10	38.1	16:30	29.8
6:40	76.7	10:00	51.1	13:20	37.8	16:40	29.5
6:50	75.5	10:10	50.4	13:30	37.2	16:50	29.1
7:00	74.0	10:20	49.5	13:40	36.8	17:00	28.9
7:10	72.6	10:30	48.6	13:50	36.3	17:10	28.5
7:20	71.3	10:40	48.0	14:00	35.9	17:20	28.3
7:30	69.9	10:50	47.4	14:10	35.5	17:30	28.0
7:40	68.3	11:00	46.6	14:20	35.1	17:40	27.7
7:50	66.8	11:10	45.8	14:30	34.7	17:50	27.4
8:00	65.2	11:20	45.1	14:40	34.3	18:00	27.1
8:10	63.9	11:30	44.4	14:50	34.0	18:10	26.8
8:20	62.5	11:40	43.7	15:00	33.6	18:20	26.6
8:30	61.2	11:50	43.2	15:10	33.1	18:30	26.3
8:40	60.2	12:00	42.3	15:20	32.7	18:40	26.0
8:50	59.1	12:10	41.7	15:30	32.2	18:50	25.7
9:00	58.1	12:20	41.0	15:40	31.8	19:00	25.4
9:10	56.9	12:30	40.4	15:50	31.4		
9:20	55.9	12:40	39.8	16:00	30.9		

Adapted from Cooper, K. H. "A Means of Assessing Maximal Oxygen Intake." *JAMA* 203:201-204, 1968; Pollock, M. L. et. al. *Health and Fitness Through Physical Activity.* New York: John Wiley and Sons, 1978: Wilmore, J. H. *Training for Sport and Activity.* Boston: Allyn and Bacon, 1982.

TABLE 2.2. Cardiovascular Fitness Classification According to Maximal Oxygen Uptake in ml/kg/min.

Sex	Age	Fitness Classification				
		Poor	Fair	Average	Good*	Excellent
Men	<29	<25	25-33	34-42	43-52	53+
	30-39	<23	23-30	31-38	39-48	49+
	40-49	<20	20-26	27-35	36-44	45+
	50-59	<18	18-24	25-33	34-42	43+
	60-69	<16	16-22	23-30	31-40	41+
Women	<29	<24	24-30	31-37	38-48	49+
	30-39	<20	20-27	28-33	34-44	45+
	40-49	<17	17-23	24-30	31-41	42+
	50-59	<15	15-20	21-27	28-37	38+
	60-69	<13	13-17	18-23	24-34	35+

*Recommended health-fitness standard

MUSCULAR STRENGTH / ENDURANCE

Many people are under the impression that muscular strength and endurance are only necessary for athletes and other individuals who hold jobs that require heavy muscular work. However, strength and endurance are important components of total physical fitness and have become an integral part of everyone's life.

Adequate levels of strength significantly enhance a person's health and well-being throughout life. Strength is crucial for optimal performance in daily activities such as sitting, walking, running, lifting and carrying objects, doing housework, or even for the enjoyment of recreational activities. Strength is also of great value in improving personal appearance and self-image, in developing sports skills, and in meeting certain emergencies in life where strength is necessary to cope effectively.

Perhaps one of the most significant benefits of maintaining a good strength level is its relationship to human metabolism. Metabolism is defined as all energy and material transformations that occur within living cells. Several studies have shown that there is a relationship between oxygen consumption as a result of metabolic activity and amount of lean body mass.

Muscle tissue uses energy even at rest, while fatty tissue uses very little energy and may be considered metabolically inert from the point of view of caloric use. As muscle size increases, so does the resting metabolism or the amount of energy (expressed in calories) required by an individual during resting conditions to sustain proper cell function. Even small increases in muscle mass increase resting metabolism.

Estimates indicate that each additional pound of muscle tissue increases resting metabolism by 50 to 100 calories per day. All other factors being equal, if one takes two individuals at 150 pounds with different amounts of muscle mass, let's say five pounds, the one with the greater muscle mass will have a higher resting metabolic rate (about 250 to 500 calories per day), thus allowing this person to eat more calories to maintain the muscle tissue.

Although muscular strength and endurance are interrelated, a basic difference exists between the two. Strength is defined as the ability of a muscle (or group of muscles) to exert maximum force against resistance. Endurance is the ability of a muscle to exert submaximal force repeatedly over a period of time. Muscular endurance depends to a large extent on muscular strength, and to a lesser extent on cardiovascular endurance. Weak muscles cannot repeat an action several times, nor sustain it for a prolonged period of time.

Muscular strength is usually determined by the maximal amount of resistance (one repetition maximum or 1 RM) that an individual is able to lift in a single effort. This assessment gives a good measure of absolute strength, but it does require a considerable amount of time to administer. Muscular endurance is commonly established by the number of repetitions that an individual can perform against a submaximal resistance or by the length of time that a given contraction can be sustained.

Muscular Endurance Test

Since we live in a world in which muscular strength and endurance are both required, and because muscular endurance depends to a large extent on muscular strength, a muscular endurance test has been selected to determine your strength level. Three exercises that will help assess the endurance of the upper body, lower body, and the abdominal/hip flexors muscle groups have been selected for your muscular endurance test. You will need a stopwatch, a metronome, a bench or gymnasium bleacher 16¼ inches high, three chairs (for men only), and a partner to perform the test.

The exercises conducted for this test are bench-jumps, chair-dips (men) or modified push-ups (women), and bent-leg curl-ups. All exercises should be conducted with the aid of a partner. The correct procedures for performing each exercise are as follows:

Bench-jumps

Using a bench or gymnasium bleacher 16¼ inches high, attempt to jump up and down the bench as many times as possible in a one-minute period (see Figure 2.2). If you cannot jump the full minute, you may step up and down. A repetition is counted each time both feet return to the floor.

FIGURE 2.2. Bench-jumps.

Chair-dips

This upper-body exercise is performed by men only. Using three sturdy chairs, place one hand each on a chair, with the fingers pointing forward. Place the feet on a third chair in front of you. The hips should be bent at approximately 90°. Lower your body by flexing the elbows until you reach a 90° angle at this joint, and then return to the starting position (see Figure 2.3). The repetition does not count if you fail to reach 90°. The repetitions are performed to a two-step cadence (down-up), regulated with a metronome set at 56 beats per minute. Perform as many continuous repetitions as possible. You can no longer count the repetitions if you fail to follow the metronome cadence.

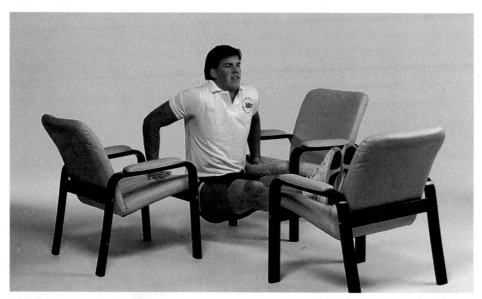

FIGURE 2.3. Chair-dips.

Modified push-ups

Women will perform the modified push-up exercise instead of the chair-dip exercise. Lie down on the floor (face down), bend the knees (feet up in the air), and place the hands on the floor by the shoulders with the fingers pointing forward. The lower body will be supported at the knees (as opposed to the feet) throughout the test (see Figure 2.4). The chest must touch the floor on each repetition. As with the chair-dip exercise, the repetitions are performed to a two-step cadence (up-down) regulated with a metronome set at 56 beats per minute. Perform as many continuous repetitions as possible. You cannot count any more repetitions if you fail to follow the metronome cadence.

FIGURE 2.4. Modified push-ups.

Bent-leg curl-ups

Lie down on the floor (face up) and bend both legs at the knees at approximately 100°. Feet should be on the floor and you must hold them in place yourself throughout the test. Cross the arms in front of your chest, each hand on the opposite shoulder. Now raise the head off the floor, placing the chin against your chest. This is the starting and finishing position for each curl-up (see Figure 2.5). **The back of the head may not come in contact with the floor, the hands cannot be removed from the shoulders, nor may the feet or hips be raised off the floor at any time during the**

FIGURE 2.5. Starting position for bent-leg curl-ups.

test. The test is terminated if any of these four conditions occur. When you curl-up, the upper body must come to an upright position before going back down (see Figure 2.6). The repetitions are performed to a two-step cadence (up-down) regulated with the metronome set at 40 beats per minute. For this exercise, you should allow a brief practice period of ten to fifteen seconds to familiarize yourself with the cadence. **The up movement is initiated with the first beat, then you must wait for the next beat to initiate the down movement — one repetition is accomplished every two beats of the metronome.** Count as many repetitions as you are able to perform following the proper cadence. This test is also terminated if you fail to maintain the appropriate cadence or if you accomplish 100 repetitions. Have your partner check the angle at the knees throughout the test to make sure that the 100° angle is maintained as closely as possible.

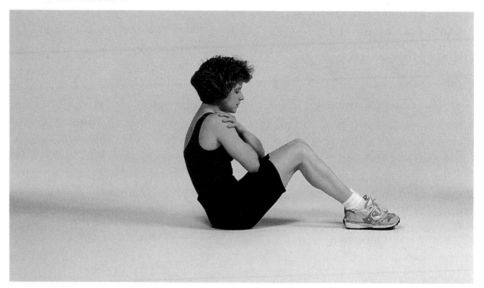

FIGURE 2.6. Upright position for bent-leg curl-ups.

According to your results, look up your percentile rank for each exercise in the far left column of Table 2.3. Next, total the percentile scores obtained for each exercise, and divide by three to obtain an average score. You can determine your individual and overall muscular endurance fitness categories according to the ratings in Table 2.4.

TABLE 2.3. Muscular Endurance Scoring Table*

MEN			
Percentile Rank	Bench Jumps	Chair Dips	Bent-leg Curl-ups
99	66	54	100
95	63	50	81
90	62	38	65
80	58	32	51
70	57	30	44
60	56	27	31
50	54	26	28
40	51	23	25
30	48	20	22
20	47	17	17
10	40	11	10
5	34	7	3
WOMEN			
Percentile Rank	Bench Jumps	Modified Push-ups	Bent-leg Curl-ups
99	58	95	100+
95	54	70	100
90	52	50	97
80	48	41	77
70	44	38	57
60	42	33	45
50	39	30	37
40	38	28	28
30	36	25	22
20	32	21	17
10	28	18	9
5	26	15	4

* Reproduced with permission from Hoeger, W. W. K. *Principles and Labs for Physical Fitness & Wellness.* Morton Publishing Company, 1988.
Shaded areas indicate the recommended health-fitness standard.

TABLE 2.4. Fitness Categories Based on Percentile Ranks.

Average Score	Endurance Classification
80+	Excellent
60–79	Good**
40–59	Average
20–39	Fair
<19	Poor

**Shaded areas indicate the recommended health-fitness standard.

MUSCULAR FLEXIBILITY

Flexibility is defined as the ability of a joint to move freely through its full range of motion. The amount of flexibility possessed by individuals is limited by factors such as joint structure, ligaments, tendons, muscles, skin, tissue injury, adipose tissue, body temperature, age, gender, and index of physical activity.

The development and maintenance of some level of flexibility are important components of everyone's health enhancement program, and even more so during the aging process. Sports medicine specialists have indicated that many muscular/skeletal problems and injuries, especially among adults, are related to a lack of flexibility.

Most experts agree that participating in a regular flexibility program will help a person maintain good joint mobility, increase resistance to muscle injury and soreness, prevent low back and other spinal column problems, improve and maintain good postural alignment, enhance proper and graceful body movement, improve personal appearance and self-image, and facilitate the development and maintenance of motor skills throughout life. Flexibility exercises have also been used successfully in the treatment of patients suffering from dysmenorrhea and general neuro-muscular tension.

Stretching exercises in conjunction with calisthenics are also helpful in warm-up routines to prepare the human body for more vigorous aerobic or strength-training exercises, as well as subsequent cool-down routines to help the organism return to the normal resting state.

Flexibility Assessment

Two flexibility tests will be used to determine your flexibility profile. These are the modified sit-and-reach test and the total body rotation test.

Modified Sit-and-Reach Test

To perform this test you will need the Acuflex I* sit-and-reach flexi-bility tester or you may simply place a yardstick on top of a box approxi-mately twelve inches high. The procedures to administer this test are as follows:

1. Be sure to properly warm up prior to the first trial.

---

* The Acuflex I and II flexibility testers for the modified sit-and-reach and the total body rotation tests can be obtained from Novel Products Figure Finder Collection, 80 Fairbanks, Unit 12, Addison, IL 60101 — (312) 628-1787.

2. Remove your shoes for the test. Sit on the floor with your hips, back, and head against a wall, legs fully extended, and the bottom of your feet against the Acuflex I or the sit-and-reach box.

3. Place your hands one on top of the other and reach forward as far as possible without letting the hips, back, or head come off the wall. Another person should then slide the reach indicator on the Acuflex I (or yardstick) along the top of the box until the end of the indicator touches the tips of your fingers (see Figure 2.7). The indicator must then be held firmly in place throughout the rest of the test.

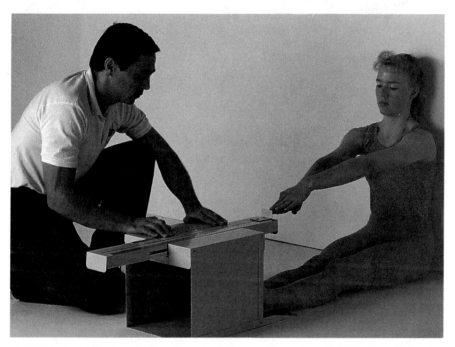

FIGURE 2.7. Determining the starting position for the Modified Sit-and-Reach Test.

4. Your head and back can now come off the wall and you may gradually reach forward three times, the third time stretching forward as far as possible on the indicator (or yardstick), holding the final position for at least two seconds (see Figure 2.8). Be sure that during the test the back of the knees are kept flat against the floor. Record the final number of inches reached to the nearest one-half inch.

FIGURE 2.8. The Modified Sit-and-Reach Test.

5. You are allowed two trials and an average of the two scores is used as the final test score. The percentile ranks and fitness categories for this test are given in Tables 2.5 and 2.4 respectively.

TABLE 2.5. Percentile Ranks for the Modified Sit-and-Reach Test*

	Percentile Rank	Age Category			
		<18	19-35	36-49	50>
	99	20.8	24.7	18.9	16.2
	95	19.6	19.5	18.2	15.8
	90	18.2	17.9	16.1	15.0
	80	17.8	17.0	14.6	13.3
	70	16.0	15.8	13.9	12.3
	60	15.2	15.0	13.4	11.5
Men	50	14.5	14.4	12.6	10.2
	40	14.0	13.5	11.6	9.7
	30	13.4	13.0	10.8	9.3
	20	11.8	11.6	9.9	8.8
	10	9.5	9.2	8.3	7.8
	05	8.4	7.9	7.0	7.2
	01	7.2	7.0	5.1	4.0
	99	22.6	19.8	19.8	17.2
	95	19.5	18.7	19.2	15.7
	90	18.7	17.9	17.4	15.0
	80	17.8	16.7	16.2	14.2
	70	16.5	16.2	15.2	13.6
	60	16.0	15.8	14.5	12.3
Women	50	15.2	14.8	13.5	11.1
	40	14.5	14.5	12.8	10.1
	30	13.7	13.7	12.2	9.2
	20	12.6	12.6	11.0	8.3
	10	11.4	10.1	9.7	7.5
	05	9.4	8.1	8.5	3.7
	01	6.5	2.6	2.0	1.5

* Reproduced with permission from Hoeger, W.W.K. *Lifetime Physical Fitness & Wellness: A Personalized Program*. Morton Publishing Company, 1989.
Shaded areas indicate the recommended health-fitness standard.

Total Body Rotation Test

An Acuflex II total body rotation flexibility tester or a measuring scale with a sliding panel is needed to administer this test. The Acuflex II or scale is placed on the wall at shoulder height and should be adjustable to accommodate individual differences in height. If you need to build your own scale, use two measuring tapes and glue them above and below the sliding panel — centered at the fifteen-inch mark. Each tape should be at least thirty inches long. If no sliding panel is available, simply tape the measuring tapes onto a wall. A line must also be drawn on the floor which is centered with the fifteen-inch mark (see Figures 2.9, 2.10, 2.11, and 2.12). The following procedures should be used for this test:

1. Be sure to properly warm up prior to initiating this test.

2. To start, you should stand sideways, an arm's length away from the wall, with the feet straight ahead, slightly separated, and the toes right up to the corresponding line drawn on the floor. The arm opposite the wall is held out horizontally from the body, making a fist with the hand. The Acuflex II, measuring scale, or tapes should be shoulder height at this time.

3. You can now rotate the body, the extended arm going backward (always maintaining a horizontal plane) and making contact with the panel, gradually sliding it forward as far as possible. If no panel is available, slide the fist alongside the tapes as far as possible. The final position must be held for at least two seconds. The hand should be positioned with the little finger side forward during the entire sliding movement, as illustrated in Figure 2.13. **It is crucial that the proper hand position be used. Many people will attempt to either open the hand, push with extended fingers, or slide the panel with the knuckles; none of which is an acceptable test procedure.** During the test, the knees can be slightly bent, but **the feet cannot be moved, always pointing straight forward.** The body must be kept as straight (vertical) as possible.

4. The test is conducted on either the right or left side of the body. You are allowed two trials on the selected side. The farthest point reached, measured to the nearest one-half inch, and held for at least two seconds is recorded. The average of the two trials is used

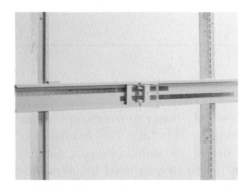

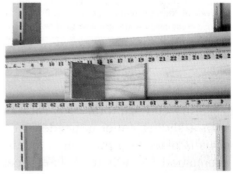

FIGURE 2.9. Acuflex II Measuring Device for the Total Body Rotation Test.

FIGURE 2.10. Homemade measuring device for the Total Body Rotation Test.

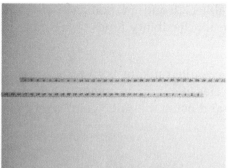

FIGURE 2.11. Use of measuring tapes for the Total Body Rotation Test.

FIGURE 2.12. Total Body Rotation Test.

FIGURE 2.13. Proper hand position for the Total Body Rotation Test.

as the final test score. Using Tables 2.6 and 2.4, you can determine the respective percentile rank and flexibility fitness classification for this test.

After obtaining your score and percentile rank for both tests, you can determine the overall flexibility fitness classification by computing an average percentile rank from the two tests and using the same guidelines given in Table 2.4.

TABLE 2.6. Percentile Ranks for the Total Body Rotation Test (Right Side)*

	Percentile Rank	Right Rotation			
		Age: <18	19-35	36-49	50>
	99	28.2	27.8	25.2	22.2
	95	25.5	25.6	23.8	20.7
	90	24.3	24.1	22.5	19.3
	80	22.7	22.3	21.0	16.3
	70	21.3	20.7	18.7	15.7
	60	19.8	19.0	17.3	14.7
Men	50	19.0	17.2	16.3	12.3
	40	17.3	16.3	14.7	11.5
	30	15.1	15.0	13.3	10.7
	20	12.9	13.3	11.2	8.7
	10	10.8	11.3	8.0	2.7
	05	8.1	8.3	5.5	0.3
	01	6.6	2.9	2.0	0.0
	99	29.6	29.4	27.1	21.7
	95	27.6	25.3	25.9	19.7
	90	25.8	23.0	21.3	19.0
	80	23.7	20.8	19.6	17.9
	70	22.0	19.3	17.3	16.8
	60	20.8	18.0	16.5	15.6
Women	50	19.5	17.3	14.6	14.0
	40	18.3	16.0	13.1	12.8
	30	16.3	15.2	11.7	8.5
	20	14.5	14.0	9.8	3.9
	10	12.4	11.1	6.1	2.2
	05	10.2	8.8	4.0	1.1
	01	8.9	3.2	2.8	0.0

*Reproduced with permission from Hoeger, W.W.K. *Lifetime Physical Fitness & Wellness: A Personalized Program.* Morton Publishintg Company, 1989.
Shaded areas indicate the recommended health-fitness standard.

TABLE 2.6 (cont.). Percentile Ranks for the Total Body Rotation Test (Left Side)*

	Percentile Rank	Age:	**Left Rotation**			
			<18	**19-35**	**36-49**	**50>**
Men	99		29.1	28.0	26.6	21.0
	95		26.6	24.8	24.5	20.0
	90		25.0	23.6	23.0	17.7
	80		22.0	22.0	21.2	15.5
	70		20.9	20.3	20.4	14.7
	60		19.9	19.3	18.7	13.9
	50		18.6	18.0	16.7	12.7
	40		17.0	16.8	15.3	11.7
	30		14.9	15.0	14.8	10.3
	20		13.8	13.3	13.7	9.5
	10		10.8	10.5	10.8	4.3
	05		8.5	8.9	8.8	0.3
	01		3.4	1.7	5.1	0.0
Women	99		29.3	28.6	27.1	23.0
	95		26.8	24.8	25.3	21.4
	90		25.5	23.0	23.4	20.5
	80		23.8	21.5	20.2	19.1
	70		21.8	20.5	18.6	17.3
	60		20.5	19.3	17.7	16.0
	50		19.5	18.0	16.4	14.8
	40		18.5	17.2	14.8	13.7
	30		17.1	15.7	13.6	10.0
	20		16.0	15.2	11.6	6.3
	10		12.8	13.6	8.5	3.0
	05		11.1	7.3	6.8	0.7
	01		8.9	5.3	4.3	0.0

* Reproduced with permission from Hoeger, W.W.K. *Lifetime Physical Fitness & Wellness: A Personalized Program.* Morton Publishing Company, 1989.
Shaded areas indicate the recommended health-fitness standard.

BODY COMPOSITION

The term "body composition" is used in reference to the fat and non-fat components of the human body. The fat component is usually referred to as fat mass or percent body fat. The nonfat component is referred to as lean body mass. Although for many years people have relied on height/weight charts to determine ideal body weight, we now know that these tables can be highly inaccurate for many people. The proper way of determining ideal weight is through body composition, that is, by finding out what percent of total body weight is fat, and what amount is lean tissue. Once the fat percentage is known, ideal body weight can be calculated from recommended body fat (see Table 2.10), or the recommended amount where there is no detriment to human health.

The importance of good body composition in the achievement and maintenance of good health cannot be underestimated. Obesity has become a health hazard of epidemic proportions in most developed countries around the world. Obesity by itself has been associated with several serious health problems and accounts for 15 to 20 percent of the annual U.S. mortality rate. Obesity has long been recognized as a major risk factor for diseases of the cardiovascular system, including coronary heart disease, hypertension, congestive heart failure, elevated blood lipids, atherosclerosis, strokes, thromboembolitic disease, varicose veins, and intermittent claudication.

While there is little disagreement regarding a greater mortality rate among obese people, scientific evidence also points to the fact that the same is true for underweight people. Although a slight change has been seen in recent years, the social pressure to achieve model-like thinness is still with us and continues to cause a gradual increase in the number of people who develop eating disorders (anorexia nervosa and bulimia, which are discussed in Chapter 4). Extreme weight loss can cause the development of such medical conditions as heart damage, gastrointestinal problems, shrinkage of internal organs, immune system abnormalities, disorders of the reproductive system, loss of muscle tissue, damage to the nervous system, and even death.

In spite of the fact that different techniques used to determine percent body fat were developed several years ago, many people are still unaware of these procedures and continue to depend on height/weight charts to find out what their "ideal" body weight should be. These standard height/weight tables were first published in 1912 and were based on average weights (including shoes and clothing) for men and women who obtained life insurance policies between 1888 and 1905. The ideal weight on the tables is obtained according to gender, height, and frame size. Since no scientific guidelines to determine frame size are given, most people choose their size based on the column where their body weight is found!

To determine whether people are truly obese or "falsely" at ideal body weight, body composition must be established. Obesity is related to excessive body fat accumulation. If body weight is used as the only criteria, an individual can easily be overweight according to height/weight charts, and yet not be obese. This is commonly seen among football players, body builders, weight lifters, and other athletes with large muscle size. Some of these athletes in reality have very little body fat but may appear to be twenty or thirty pounds overweight.

On the other end of the spectrum, some people who weigh very little and are viewed by many as "skinny" or underweight can actually be classified as obese because of their high body fat content. Not at all uncommon are cases of people weighing as little as 100 pounds who are over 30 percent fat (about one-third of their total body weight). Such cases are more readily observed among sedentary people and those who are constantly dieting. Both physical inactivity and constant negative caloric balance lead to a loss in lean body mass. It is clear from these examples that body weight alone does not always tell the true story.

Total fat in the human body is classified into two types, essential fat and storage fat. The essential fat is needed for normal physiological functions, and without it, human health begins to deteriorate. This essential fat constitutes about 3 percent of the total weight in men and about 12 percent in women. The percentage is higher in women because it includes sex-specific fat, such as found in the breast tissue, the uterus, and other sex-related fat deposits. Storage fat constitutes the fat that is stored in adipose tissue, mostly beneath the skin (subcutaneous fat) and around major organs in the body.

Body Composition Assessment Through Skinfold Thickness

The assessment of body composition is most frequently done using skinfold thickness. This technique is based on the principle that approximately 50 percent of the fatty tissue in the body is deposited directly beneath the skin. If this tissue is estimated validly and reliably, a good indication of percent body fat can be obtained. This test is regularly performed with the aid of pressure calipers* (see Figure 2.14), and several sites must be measured to reflect the total percentage of fat. These sites are triceps, suprailium, and thigh skinfolds for women; and chest, abdomen, and thigh for men. All measurements should be taken on the right side of the body with the subject standing. The correct anatomical landmarks for skinfolds are (see Figure 2.15):

Chest: a diagonal fold halfway between the shoulder crease and the nipple.

Abdomen: a vertical fold about one inch to the right of the umbilicus.

---

* An inexpensive, yet reliable skinfold caliper can be obtained from Fat Control, Inc., P.O. Box 10117, Towson, MD 21204 — Phone (301) 296-1993

Triceps: a vertical fold on the back of the upper arm, halfway between the shoulder and the arm.

Thigh: a diagonal fold on the front of the thigh, midway between the knee and the hip.

Suprailium: a diagonal fold above the crest of the ilium (on the side of the hip).

FIGURE 2.14. Skinfold thickness technique for body composition assessment.

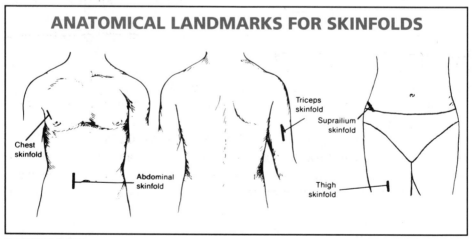

FIGURE 2.15.

Each site is measured by grasping a double thickness of skin firmly with the thumb and forefinger, pulling the fold slightly away from the muscle tissue. Hold the calipers perpendicular to the fold, and take the measurements one-half inch below the finger hold. Measure each site three times and read the values to the nearest .1 to .5 mm. Record the average of the two closest readings as the final value. Take the readings without delay to avoid excessive compression of the skinfold. Releasing and refolding the skinfold is required between readings. After determining the average value for each site, percent fat can be obtained by adding together all three skin-fold measurements and looking up the respective values in Tables 2.7 for women, 2.8 for men under forty, and 2.9 for men over forty. You may then proceed to compute your ideal body weight using the recommended percent body fat range given in Table 2.10 and the computation form in Figure 2.16.

The reader should keep in mind that the recommended percent body fat values given in Table 2.10 include essential fat and storage fat, previously discussed in this chapter. For example, the recommended body fat range for women under thirty is 17 to 25 percent. This indicates that only 5 to 13 percent of the total recommended fat is storage fat, while the other 12 percent is in the form of essential fat. The recommended range has been selected based on research which indicates that some storage fat is required for optimal health and greater longevity. The range selected in this book also includes the recommendations made by most health and fitness experts throughout the United States. If you desire to have just "one" target weight, you may select your body weight based on your personal preference, as long as it falls within the recommended range.

You should also realize that if you engage in a diet/exercise program, it is recommended that you repeat the computations about once a month to monitor changes in body composition. This is important, because lean body mass is affected by weight reduction programs as well as by physical activity. A negative caloric balance does lead to a decrease in lean body mass (these effects will be explained in more detail in Chapter 4). As lean body mass changes, so will your ideal body weight.

An example of the changes in body composition resulting from a weight control/exercise program was seen in a coed aerobic dance course taught at The University of Texas of the Permian Basin in Odessa, Texas. The class was taught during a six-week summer term, and students participated in aerobic dance routines four times per week for sixty minutes each time. The first and last day of classes were used to assess several physiological parameters, including body composition. Students were also given information on diet and nutrition and basically followed their own weight control program. At the end of the six weeks, the average weight loss for

TABLE 2.7. Percent fat estimates for women calculated from triceps, suprailium, and thigh skinfold thickness.

Sum of 3 Skinfolds	Under 22	23 to 27	28 to 32	33 to 37	38 to 42	43 to 47	48 to 52	53 to 57	Over 58
					Age to the Last Year				
23-25	9.7	9.9	10.2	10.4	10.7	10.9	11.2	11.4	11.7
26-28	11.0	11.2	11.5	11.7	12.0	12.3	12.5	12.7	13.0
29-31	12.3	12.5	12.8	13.0	13.3	13.5	13.8	14.0	14.3
32-34	13.6	13.8	14.0	14.3	14.5	14.8	15.0	15.3	15.5
35-37	14.8	15.0	15.3	15.5	15.8	16.0	16.3	16.5	16.8
38-40	16.0	16.3	16.5	16.7	17.0	17.2	17.5	17.7	18.0
41-43	17.2	17.4	17.7	17.9	18.2	18.4	18.7	18.9	19.2
44-46	18.3	18.6	18.8	19.1	19.3	19.6	19.8	20.1	20.3
47-49	19.5	19.7	20.0	20.2	20.5	20.7	21.0	21.2	21.5
50-52	20.6	20.8	21.1	21.3	21.6	21.8	22.1	22.3	22.6
53-55	21.7	21.9	22.1	22.4	22.6	22.9	23.1	23.4	23.6
56-58	22.7	23.0	23.2	23.4	23.7	23.9	24.2	24.4	24.7
59-61	23.7	24.0	24.2	24.5	24.7	25.0	25.2	25.5	25.7
62-64	24.7	25.0	25.2	25.5	25.7	26.0	26.2	26.4	26.7
65-67	25.7	25.9	26.2	26.4	26.7	26.9	27.2	27.4	27.7
68-70	26.6	26.9	27.1	27.4	27.6	27.9	28.1	28.4	28.6
71-73	27.5	27.8	28.0	28.3	28.5	28.8	29.0	29.3	29.5
74-76	28.4	28.7	28.9	29.2	29.4	29.7	29.9	30.2	30.4
77-79	29.3	29.5	29.8	30.0	30.3	30.5	30.8	31.0	31.3

80- 82	30.1	30.4	30.6	30.9	31.1	31.4	31.6	31.9	32.1
83- 85	30.9	31.2	31.4	31.7	31.9	32.2	32.4	32.7	32.9
86- 88	31.7	32.0	32.2	32.5	32.7	32.9	33.2	33.4	33.7
89- 91	32.5	32.7	33.0	33.2	33.5	33.7	33.9	34.2	34.4
92- 94	33.2	33.4	33.7	33.9	34.2	34.4	34.7	34.9	35.2
95- 97	33.9	34.1	34.4	34.6	34.9	35.1	35.4	35.6	35.9
98-100	34.6	34.8	35.1	35.3	35.5	35.8	36.0	36.3	36.5
101-103	35.2	35.4	35.7	35.9	36.2	36.4	36.7	36.9	37.2
104-106	35.8	36.1	36.3	36.6	36.8	37.1	37.3	37.5	37.8
107-109	36.4	36.7	36.9	37.1	37.4	37.6	37.9	38.1	38.4
110-112	37.0	37.2	37.5	37.7	38.0	38.2	38.5	38.7	38.9
113-115	37.5	37.8	38.0	38.2	38.5	38.7	39.0	39.2	39.5
116-118	38.0	38.3	38.5	38.8	39.0	39.3	39.5	39.7	40.0
119-121	38.5	38.7	39.0	39.2	39.5	39.7	40.0	40.2	40.5
122-124	39.0	39.2	39.4	39.7	39.9	40.2	40.4	40.7	40.9
125-127	39.4	39.6	39.9	40.1	40.4	40.6	40.9	41.1	41.4
128-130	39.8	40.0	40.3	40.5	40.8	41.0	41.3	41.5	41.8

Body density calculated based on the generalized equation for predicting body density of women developed by Jackson, A. S., M. L. Pollock. *BritishJournal of Nutrition* 40:497-504, 1978. Percent body fat determined from the calculated body density using the Siri formula (W. E. Siri, *Body Composition from Fluid Spaces and Density.* Berkeley, CA; University of California, Donner Laboratory of Medical Physics, 1956).

Table 2.8. Percent fat estimates for men under 40 calculated from chest, abdomen, and thigh skinfold thickness.

Sum of 3 Skinfolds	Age to the Last Year							
	Under 19	20 to 22	23 to 25	26 to 28	29 to 31	32 to 34	35 to 37	38 to 40
8- 10	.9	1.3	1.6	2.0	2.3	2.7	3.0	3.3
11- 13	1.9	2.3	2.6	3.0	3.3	3.7	4.0	4.3
14- 16	2.9	3.3	3.6	3.9	4.3	4.6	5.0	5.3
17- 19	3.9	4.2	4.6	4.9	5.3	5.6	6.0	6.3
20- 22	4.8	5.2	5.5	5.9	6.2	6.6	6.9	7.3
23- 25	5.8	6.2	6.5	6.8	7.2	7.5	7.9	8.2
26- 28	6.8	7.1	7.5	7.8	8.1	8.5	8.8	9.2
29- 31	7.7	8.0	8.4	8.7	9.1	9.4	9.8	10.1
32- 34	8.6	9.0	9.3	9.7	10.0	10.4	10.7	11.1
35- 37	9.5	9.9	10.2	10.6	10.9	11.3	11.6	12.0
38- 40	10.5	10.8	11.2	11.5	11.8	12.2	12.5	12.9
41- 43	11.4	11.7	12.1	12.4	12.7	13.1	13.4	13.8
44- 46	12.2	12.6	12.9	13.3	13.6	14.0	14.3	14.7
47- 49	13.1	13.5	13.8	14.2	14.5	14.9	15.2	15.5
50- 52	14.0	14.3	14.7	15.0	15.4	15.7	16.1	16.4
53- 55	14.8	15.2	15.5	15.9	16.2	16.6	16.9	17.3
56- 58	15.7	16.0	16.4	16.7	17.1	17.4	17.8	18.1
59- 61	16.5	16.9	17.2	17.6	17.9	18.3	18.6	19.0
62- 64	17.4	17.7	18.1	18.4	18.8	19.1	19.4	19.8

Weight (lb)								
65- 67	18.2	18.5	18.9	19.2	19.6	19.9	20.3	20.6
68- 70	19.0	19.3	19.7	20.0	20.4	20.7	21.1	21.4
71- 73	19.8	20.1	20.5	20.8	21.2	21.5	21.9	22.2
74- 76	20.6	20.9	21.3	21.6	22.0	22.2	22.7	23.0
77- 79	21.4	21.7	22.1	22.4	22.8	23.1	23.4	23.8
80- 82	22.1	22.5	22.8	23.2	23.5	23.9	24.2	24.6
83- 85	22.9	23.2	23.6	23.9	24.3	24.6	25.0	25.3
86- 88	23.6	24.0	24.3	24.7	25.0	25.4	25.7	26.1
89- 91	24.4	24.7	25.1	25.4	25.8	26.1	26.5	26.8
92- 94	25.1	25.5	25.8	26.2	26.5	26.9	27.2	27.5
95- 97	25.8	26.2	26.5	26.9	27.2	27.6	27.9	28.3
98-100	26.6	26.9	27.3	27.6	27.9	28.3	28.6	29.0
101-103	27.3	27.6	28.0	28.3	28.6	29.0	29.3	29.7
104-106	27.9	28.3	28.6	29.0	29.3	29.7	30.0	30.4
107-109	28.6	29.0	29.3	29.7	30.0	30.4	30.7	31.1
110-112	29.3	29.6	30.0	30.3	30.7	31.0	31.4	31.7
113-115	30.0	30.3	30.7	31.0	31.3	31.7	32.0	32.4
116-118	30.6	31.0	31.3	31.6	32.0	32.3	32.7	33.0
119-121	31.3	31.6	32.0	32.3	32.6	33.0	33.3	33.7
122-124	31.9	32.2	32.6	32.9	33.3	33.6	34.0	34.3
125-127	32.5	32.9	33.2	33.5	33.9	34.2	34.6	34.9
128-130	33.1	33.5	33.8	34.2	34.5	34.9	35.2	35.5

Body density calculated based on the generalized equation for predicting body density of men developed by Jackson, A.S., and M. L. Pollock. *British Journal of Nutrition* 40:497-504, 1978. Percent body fat determined from the calculated body density using the Siri formula (W. E. Siri, *Body Composition from Fluid Spaces and Density*. Berkeley, CA; University of California, Donner Laboratory of Medical Physics, 1956).

Table 2.9. Percent fat estimates for men over 40 calculated from chest, abdomen, and thigh skinfold thickness.

Sum of 3 Skinfolds	Age to the Last Year							
	41 to 43	44 to 46	47 to 49	50 to 52	53 to 55	56 to 58	59 to 61	Over 62
8-10	3.7	4.0	4.4	4.7	5.1	5.4	5.8	6.1
11-13	4.7	5.0	5.4	5.7	6.1	6.4	6.8	7.1
14-16	5.7	6.0	6.4	6.7	7.1	7.4	7.8	8.1
17-19	6.7	7.0	7.4	7.7	8.1	8.4	8.7	9.1
20-22	7.6	8.0	8.3	8.7	9.0	9.4	9.7	10.1
23-25	8.6	8.9	9.3	9.6	10.0	10.3	10.7	11.0
26-28	9.5	9.9	10.2	10.6	10.9	11.3	11.6	12.0
29-31	10.5	10.8	11.2	11.5	11.9	12.2	12.6	12.9
32-34	11.4	11.8	12.1	12.4	12.8	13.1	13.5	13.8
35-37	12.3	12.7	13.0	13.4	13.7	14.1	14.4	14.8
38-40	13.2	13.6	13.9	14.3	14.6	15.0	15.3	15.7
41-43	14.1	14.5	14.8	15.2	15.5	15.9	16.2	16.6
44-46	15.0	15.4	15.7	16.1	16.4	16.8	17.1	17.5
47-49	15.9	16.2	16.6	16.9	17.3	17.6	18.0	18.3
50-52	16.8	17.1	17.5	17.8	18.2	18.5	18.8	19.2
53-55	17.6	18.0	18.3	18.7	19.0	19.4	19.7	20.1
56-58	18.5	18.8	19.2	19.5	19.9	20.2	20.6	20.9
59-61	19.3	19.7	20.0	20.4	20.7	21.0	21.4	21.7
62-64	20.1	20.5	20.8	21.2	21.5	21.9	22.2	22.6

65- 67	21.0	21.3	21.7	22.0	22.4	22.7	23.0	23.4
68- 70	21.8	22.1	22.5	22.8	23.2	23.5	23.9	24.2
71- 73	22.6	22.9	23.3	23.6	24.0	24.3	24.7	25.0
74- 76	23.4	23.7	24.1	24.4	24.8	25.1	25.4	25.8
77- 79	24.1	24.5	24.8	25.2	25.5	25.9	26.2	26.6
80- 82	24.9	25.3	25.6	26.0	26.3	26.6	27.0	27.3
83- 85	25.7	26.0	26.4	26.7	27.1	27.4	27.8	28.1
86- 88	26.4	26.8	27.1	27.5	27.8	28.2	28.5	28.9
89- 91	27.2	27.5	27.9	38.2	28.6	28.9	29.2	29.6
92- 94	27.9	28.2	28.6	28.9	29.3	29.6	30.0	30.3
95- 97	28.6	29.0	29.3	29.7	30.0	30.4	30.7	31.1
98-100	29.3	29.7	30.0	30.4	30.7	31.1	31.4	31.8
101-103	30.0	30.4	30.7	31.1	31.4	31.8	32.1	32.5
104-106	30.7	31.1	31.4	31.8	32.1	32.5	32.8	33.2
107-109	31.4	31.8	32.1	32.4	32.8	33.1	33.5	33.8
110-112	32.1	32.4	32.8	33.1	33.5	33.8	34.2	34.5
113-115	32.7	33.1	33.4	33.8	34.1	34.5	34.8	35.2
116-118	33.4	33.7	34.1	34.4	34.8	35.1	35.5	35.8
119-121	34.0	34.4	34.7	35.1	35.4	35.8	36.1	36.5
122-124	34.7	35.0	35.4	35.7	36.1	36.4	36.7	37.1
125-127	35.3	35.6	36.0	36.3	36.7	37.0	37.4	37.7
128-130	35.9	36.2	36.6	36.9	37.3	37.6	38.0	38.35

Body density calculated based on the generalized equation for predicting body density of men developed by Jackson, A. S., and M. L. Pollock. *British Journal of Nutrition* 40:497-504, 1978. Percent body fat determined from the calculated body density using the Siri formula (W. E. Siri, *Body Composition from Fluid Spaces and Density.* Berkeley, CA: University of California, Donner Laboratory of Medical Physics, 1956).

the entire class was only three pounds. Because body composition was assessed, however, members of the class were surprised to find out that in reality the average fat loss was six pounds, accompanied by a three-pound increase in lean body mass.

TABLE 2.10. Recommended body composition according to percent body fat.

Age	Males	Females
<29	12–20%	17–25%
30-49	13–21%	18–26%
50>	14–22%	19–27%

A. Current Body Weight (BW): _____ 95 _____ lbs

B. Current Percent Fat (%F)*: _____ 20.3 %

C. Fat Weight (FW) = BW × %F = _____ × _____ = _____ lbs

D. Lean Body Mass (LBM) = BW − FW = _____ = _____ = _____ lbs

E. Age: _____

F. Recommended Fat Percent (RFP) Range (see Table 2.10): ____to ____ %

   Low End of Recommended Fat Percent Range (LRFP): _____%

   High End of Recommended Fat Percent Range (HRFP): _____%

G. Ideal Body Weight Range

   Low End of Ideal Body Weight Range (LIBW) = LBM/(1.0 − LRFP)

   LRBW = _____ / (1.0 − _____) = _____ lbs

   High End of Ideal Body Weight Range (HIBW) = LBM/(1.0 − HRFP)

   HRBW = _____ / (1.0 − _____) = _____ lbs

   Ideal Body Weight Range: _____ to _____ lbs

*Express percentages in decimal form (e.g., 25% = .25)

FIGURE 2.16. Recommended body weight determination.

Exercise Prescription | 3

A most inspiring story illustrating what fitness can do for a person's health and well-being is that of George Snell from Sandy, Utah. At the age of forty-five, Snell weighed approximately 400 pounds, his blood pressure was 220/180, he was blind because of diabetes that he did not know he had, and his blood glucose level was 487. Snell had determined to do something about his physical and medical condition, so he started a walking/jogging program. After about eight months of conditioning, Snell had lost almost 200 pounds, his eyesight had returned, his glucose level was down to 67, and he was taken off medication. Two months later, less than ten months after initiating his personal exercise program, he completed his first marathon, a running course of 26.2 miles.

Results of epidemiological research studies have established that participating in a lifetime exercise program greatly contributes toward the enhancement and maintenance of good health. There are, nonetheless, too many individuals who exercise regularly, but when they take a battery of fitness tests are surprised to find that they may not be as conditioned as they thought they were. Although these individuals may be exercising regularly, they most likely are not following the basic principles for exercise prescription; therefore, they do not reap significant benefits.

A key principle in exercise prescription is that all programs must be individualized to obtain optimal results. The reader must realize that our bodies are not all alike and that fitness levels and needs vary among individuals. The information presented in this chapter, therefore, has been developed to provide you with the necessary guidelines to write a personalized cardiovascular, strength, and flexibility exercise program to promote and maintain physical fitness. Information on weight control to achieve ideal body composition, the fourth component of physical fitness, is given in Chapter 4.

CARDIOVASCULAR ENDURANCE

Cardiovascular endurance has been defined as the ability of the heart, lungs, and blood vessels to supply oxygen and nutrients to the cells to meet the demands of prolonged physical activity (aerobic exercise). Whereas there are four components of physical fitness, cardiovascular endurance is the single most important factor. Adequate amounts of muscular strength and flexibility are necessary in daily activities to lead a

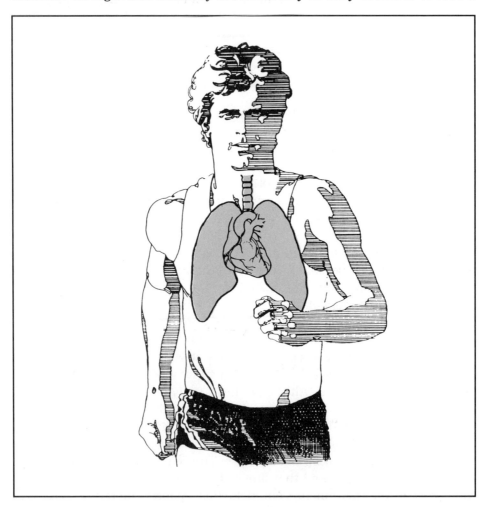

FIGURE 3.1. Cardiovascular endurance. The ability of the heart, lungs, and blood vessels to deliver adequate amounts of oxygen and nutrients to the cells to meet the demands of prolonged physical activity.

normal life. However, a person can go through life without large amounts of strength and flexibility but cannot do without a good cardiovascular system.

Aerobic exercise is especially important in the prevention of coronary heart disease. A poorly conditioned cardiovascular system is subject to more wear-and-tear than a well-conditioned system. In situations where strenuous demands are placed on the heart, such as doing yard work, lifting heavy objects, shovelling snow, or experiencing undue stress, the unconditioned heart may not be able to sustain the strain. Additionally, regular participation in cardiovascular endurance activities helps achieve and maintain ideal body weight, the fourth component of physical fitness.

Principles of Cardiovascular Exercise Prescription

The objective of aerobic training is to improve the capacity of the cardiovascular system. To accomplish this improvement, the heart muscle has to be overloaded like any other muscle in the human body, which is accomplished through aerobic exercise. Just as the biceps muscle in the upper arm is developed by doing strength-training exercises, the heart muscle also has to be exercised to increase in size, strength, and efficiency. To better understand how the cardiovascular system is developed, the four basic principles that govern this development will be discussed. These principles are intensity, mode, duration, and frequency of exercise.

Intensity of Exercise

This principle refers to how hard a person has to exercise to improve cardiovascular endurance. While the training stimuli to develop the biceps muscle can be accomplished with arm curl exercises, the stimuli for the cardiovascular system is provided by making the heart pump at a higher rate for a certain period of time. Research has shown that cardiovascular development occurs when working at about 60 to 90 percent of the heart's reserve capacity. Many experts, however, prefer to prescribe exercise between 70 and 85 percent of this capacity. This is done to insure better and faster development (70 percent) and for safety reasons (85 percent), so that unconditioned individuals will not work too close to maximum capacity. The 70 and 85 percentages can be easily calculated and training can be monitored by checking your pulse. The following steps are used to determine the intensity of exercise or cardiovascular training zone:

A. Estimate your maximal heart rate (MHR). This is done using the following formula:

MHR = 220 minus age (220 − age)

B. Take your resting heart rate (RHR). RHR is determined by counting your pulse on the wrist by placing two or three fingers over the radial artery (forearm on the side of the thumb) or over the carotid artery in the neck just below the jaw next to your voice box — see Figures 3.2 and 3.3). Count your pulse for one full minute to obtain your resting heart rate. Always start counting with zero.

FIGURE 3.2. Pulse taken at the radial artery.

FIGURE 3.3. Pulse taken at the carotid artery.

C. Determine the heart rate reserve (HRR). This is accomplished by subtracting the RHR from the maximal heart rate (HRR = MHR − RHR).

D. The target training zone is determined by computing the training intensities (TI) at 70 and 85 percent. Multiply the heart rate reserve by the respective 70 and 85 percentages and then add the resting heart rate to both of these figures (70 percent TI = HRR × .70 + RHR, and 85 percent TI = HRR × .85 + RHR). Your target training zone is found between these two target heart rates.

E. *Example.* The cardiovascular training zone for a twenty-year-old person with a resting heart rate of 72 bpm would be:

MHR: 220 − 20 = 200 bpm
RHR = 72 bpm

HRR: 200 − 72 = 128 beats
70 Percent TI = (128 × .70) + 72 = 162 bpm
85 Percent TI = (128 × .85) + 72 = 181 bpm
Cardiovascular training zone: 162 to 181 bpm

The target training zone indicates that whenever you exercise to improve the cardiovascular system, you have to maintain the heart rate between the 70 and 85 percent training intensities to obtain adequate development. If you have been physically inactive, you may want to use a 60 percent training intensity during the first four to six weeks of your exercise program. Using the previous equation, the 60 percent training intensity is obtained by multiplying your HRR by .60 and then adding the RHR to this figure. Following the initial conditioning period, you can move up to the target training zone (70 to 85 percent level).

After a few weeks of training, you should also experience a significant reduction in resting heart rate (ten to twenty beats in eight to twelve weeks); therefore, you should recompute your target zone periodically. You can compute your own cardiovascular training zone by using the form provided in Figure 3.4.

The reader should also realize that to develop the cardiovascular system you do not have to exercise above the 85 percent rate. From a health standpoint, training above this percentage will not add any extra benefits, but may actually be unsafe for some individuals. For unconditioned adults it is recommended that cardiovascular training be conducted around the 70 percent rate. This lower rate is recommended to reduce potential problems associated with high-intensity exercise.

Mode of Exercise

The type of exercise that develops the cardiovascular system has to be aerobic in nature. Once you have established your cardiovascular training zone, any activity or combination of activities that will get your heart rate up to that training zone and keep it there for as long as you exercise will yield adequate development. Examples of such activities are walking, jogging, aerobic dancing, water aerobics, swimming, cross-country skiing, rope skipping, cycling, racquetball, stair climbing, and stationary running or cycling.

Duration of Exercise

Regarding the duration of exercise, it is recommended that a person maintain the heart rate in the target training zone between fifteen and sixty minutes per session. The duration is based on how intensely a person trains. If the training is done around 85 percent of HRR, fifteen to twenty

Intensity of Exercise

1. Estimate your own maximal heart rate (MHR). Use 220 minus age (220 − age.)

   MHR = 220 − ___~~19~~___ = ___~~201~~___ bpm

2. Resting Heart Rate (RHR) = ___~~90~~ 72___ bpm

3. Heart Rate Reserve (HRR) = MHR − RHR

   HRR = ___~~201~~ 202___ − ___~~72~~___ = ___129___ beats

4. Training Intensity (TI) = HRR × %TI + RHR

   60 Percent TI = ___129 / 202___ × .60 + ___~~90~~___ = ___137___ bpm

   70 Percent TI = ___112 / 202___ × .70 + ___90___ = ___168___ bpm

   85 Percent TI = ___112 / 202___ × .85 + ___90___ = ___185___ bpm

5. Cardiovascular Training Zone. The optimum cardiovascular training zone is found between the 70 and 85 percent training intensities. However, individuals that have been physically inactive or are in the poor or fair cardiovascular fitness categories should use a 60 percent training intensity during the first few weeks of the exercise program.

   Cardiovascular Training Zone: ___162.4___ (70% TI) to ___182.2___ (85% TI)

Mode of Exercise: List any activity or combination of aerobic activities that you will use in your cardiovascular training program.

___Run, aerobics ~~biking~~/aerobics___

Duration of Exercise: Indicate the length of your exercise sessions.

___~~20min or 60min~~ 60min.___

Frequency of Exercise: Indicate the days that you will exercise.

___~~5 days a week~~ 3-4 days a week___

Student Name: _____ Date: _____

Signature: _____

Instructor's Signature: _____

FIGURE 3.4. Cardiovascular exercise prescription form.

minutes are sufficient. At 60 to 70 percent intensity, the person should train for at least thirty minutes.

Frequency of Exercise

Ideally, a person should engage in aerobic exercise four or five days per week. Research has indicated that to maintain cardiovascular fitness, a training session should be conducted about every forty-eight hours. Three twenty- to thirty-minute training sessions per week, done on nonconsecutive days, will maintain cardiovascular endurance as long as the heart rate is in the appropriate target zone.

Tips to Enhance Your Aerobic Workout

A typical aerobic workout is usually divided into three parts (see Figure 3.5): (a) a two- to five-minute warm-up phase during which the heart rate is gradually increased to the target zone; (b) the actual aerobic workout, where the heart rate is maintained in the target zone for fifteen to sixty minutes; and (c) the aerobic cool-down, where the heart rate is gradually lowered toward the resting level. It is important that you not stop abruptly following aerobic exercise. This will cause blood to pool in the exercised body parts, thereby diminishing the return of blood to the heart. A decreased blood return can cause dizziness, faintness, or even induce cardiac abnormalities.

To monitor the target training zone, you will need to know how to take your exercise heart rate. This is also done by checking your pulse on the radial or the carotid artery. Caution should be used when taking the pulse at the carotid artery because too much pressure on the artery may slow the heart and the measurement will be inaccurate. When you check the heart rate, begin with zero and count the number of beats in a ten second period, then multiply by six to get the per-minute pulse rate. Exercise heart rate should not be taken for a full minute because the heart rate begins to slow down fifteen seconds following exercise cessation. Since it is difficult to feel the pulse while exercising, do not hesitate to stop during your exercise bout to check your pulse. If the rate is too low, increase the intensity of the exercise. If the rate is too high, slow down. You may want to practice taking your pulse several times during the day to become familiar with these monitoring techniques.

For the first few weeks of your program, heart rate should be monitored several times during the exercise session. As you become familiar with your body's response to exercise, you may only have to monitor the heart rate twice: once at five to seven minutes into your exercise session, and a second time near the end of the workout.

Fitness and Wellness

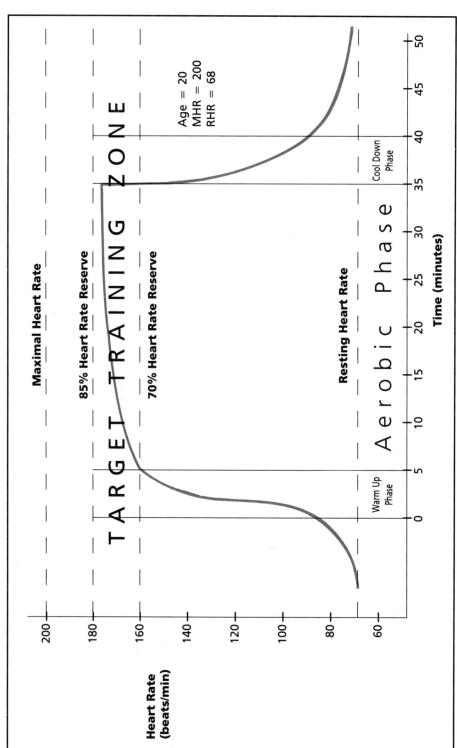

FIGURE 3.5. Typical aerobic workout pattern.

Another technique that is sometimes used to determine your exercise intensity is by talking during exercise and then taking the pulse immediately thereafter. Learning to associate the degree of difficulty when talking to the actual exercise heart rate will allow you to develop a sense of how hard you are working. Generally, if you can talk easily, you are not working hard enough. If you can talk but are slightly breathless, you should be close to the target range. If you cannot talk at all, you are working too hard.

A final point to consider during any exercise program is that you need to learn to listen to your body. There will be times when you will feel unusually fatigued or experience excessive discomfort. Pain is nature's way of letting you know that something is wrong. If you experience pain or undue discomfort during or following exercise, you need to slow down or discontinue your exercise program and notify the course instructor. Your instructor may be able to pinpoint the reason for the discomfort or recommend that you consult your physician. You are also going to be able to prevent potential injuries by paying attention to pain signals and making adjustments accordingly.

MUSCULAR STRENGTH AND ENDURANCE

Muscular strength has been defined as the ability to exert maximum force against resistance, while muscular endurance is the ability of a muscle to exert submaximal force repeatedly over a period of time. As was mentioned in Chapter 2, adequate levels of strength and endurance are necessary for optimal performance in daily activities such as sitting, walking, running, lifting and carrying objects, doing housework, or even for the enjoyment of recreational activities. Adequate strength and endurance also help decrease the risk of injury. Furthermore, greater muscle tone increases resting metabolic rate, which in the long run, helps with weight reduction and/or weight maintenance.

Over the years it has been well documented that muscle cells will increase and decrease their capacity to exert force according to the demands placed upon the muscular system. If specific muscle cells are overloaded beyond their normal use, such as in strength-training programs, the cells will increase in size (hypertrophy), strength, and/or endurance. If the demands placed on the muscle cells decrease, such as in sedentary living or required rest due to illness or injury, the cells will decrease in size (atrophy) and lose strength.

Overload Principle

The overload principle states that for strength and/or endurance improvements to occur, the demands placed on the muscle must be systematically and progressively increased over a period of time, and the resistance must be of a magnitude significant enough to cause physiologic adaptation. In simpler terms, just like all other organs and systems of the human body, muscles have to be taxed beyond their regular accustomed loads to increase in physical capacity.

Specificity of Training

Another important aspect of training is the concept of specificity of training. This principle indicates that for a muscle to increase in strength or endurance, the training program must be specific to obtain the desired effects. In like manner, to increase isometric (static) versus isotonic (dynamic) strength, an individual must use the corresponding static or dynamic training procedures to achieve the appropriate results. If a person is trying to improve a particular movement or skill through strength increases, the selected strength-training exercises must resemble the actual movement or skill as close as possible.

Principles of Strength-Training Prescription

Similar to the prescription of cardiovascular exercise, several principles need to be observed to improve muscular strength and endurance. These principles are mode, resistance, sets, and frequency of training.

Mode of Training

Two basic types of training methods are used to improve strength: isometric and isotonic. Isometric or static training refers to a muscular contraction producing little or no movement, such as pushing or pulling against immovable objects. Isotonic or dynamic training refers to a muscular contraction with movement, such as lifting an object over the head. Isotonic training programs can be conducted without weights or with free weights (barbells and dumbbells), fixed resistance machines, variable resistance machines, and isokinetic equipment.

When a person performs isotonic exercises without weights (e.g., pull-ups, push-ups), with free weights, or with fixed resistance machines, a constant resistance (weight) is moved through a joint's full range of motion. The greatest resistance (weight) that can be lifted equals the maximum weight that can be moved at the weakest angle of the joint. This is due to changes in muscle length and angle of pull as the joint moves through its range of motion.

As the popularity of strength training increased, new strength-training machines were developed. This new technology brought about the introduction of isokinetic and variable resistance training. These training programs require the use of special machines equipped with mechanical devices that provide a variable resistance, with the intent of overloading the muscle group maximally through the entire range of motion. A distinction of isokinetic training is that the speed of the muscular contraction is kept constant because the machine provides an accommodating resistance to match the user's force through the range of motion.

The mode of training used by an individual depends largely on the type of equipment available and the specific objective that the training program is attempting to accomplish. Isometric training does not require much equipment and was commonly used several years ago, but its popularity has significantly decreased in recent years. Since strength gains with isometric training are specific to the angle at which the contraction is being performed, this type of training is beneficial in a sport like gymnastics, where static contractions (e.g., handstands, iron cross, "L" supports) are regularly used during routines.

Isotonic training is the most popular mode used in strength training. The primary advantage is that strength gains occur through the full range of motion. Most daily activities are isotonic in nature. We are constantly lifting, pushing, and pulling objects, where strength is needed through a complete range of motion. Another advantage is that improvements are easily measured by the amount lifted.

The benefits of isokinetic and variable resistance training are similar to the other isotonic training methods. Theoretically, strength gains should be better because maximum resistance is applied at all angles. However, research has not shown this type of training to be more effective than other modes of isotonic training. A possible advantage is that specific speeds used in various sport skills can be more closely duplicated with isokinetic strength training, which may enhance performance (specificity of training). A disadvantage is that the equipment is not readily available to many people.

Resistance

Resistance in strength training is the equivalent of intensity in cardiovascular exercise prescription. The amount of resistance used, or weight that is lifted, depends on whether the individual is trying to develop muscular strength or muscular endurance.

To stimulate strength development, a resistance of approximately 80 percent of the maximum capacity (1 RM) must be used. For example, a person who can press 150 pounds should work with at least 120 pounds (150 × .80). Using less than 80 percent will help increase muscular endurance rather than strength. Because of the time factor involved in constantly determining the 1 RM on each lift to insure that the person is indeed working above 80 percent, a rule of thumb widely accepted by many authors and coaches is that individuals should perform between three and ten repetitions maximum for adequate strength gains. In other words, if a person is training with a resistance of 120 pounds and cannot lift it more than ten times, training stimuli are adequate for strength development. Once the weight can be lifted more than ten times, the resistance should be increased by five to ten pounds and the person should again build up to ten repetitions. If training is conducted with more than ten repetitions, muscular endurance will be primarily developed.

Strength research indicates that the closer a person trains to the 1 RM, the greater the strength gains. A disadvantage of constantly working at or near the 1 RM is that it increases the risk of injury. Three to six repetitions maximum are frequently used by highly trained athletes seeking maximum strength development. From a health-fitness point of view, six to ten repetitions maximum are ideal for adequate development. We live in an "isotonic world" in which muscular strength and endurance are both required to lead an enjoyable life; therefore, working near the ten-repetition threshold seems best to improve overall performance.

Sets

A set in strength training has been defined as the number of repetitions performed for a given exercise. For example, a person lifting 120 pounds eight times has performed one set of eight repetitions. The number of sets recommended for optimum development is anywhere from three to five sets, with about ninety seconds recovery time between each set. Due to the physiology of muscle fiber, there is a limit to the number of sets that can be done. As the number of sets increases, so does the amount of muscular fatigue and subsequent recovery time; therefore, strength gains may be lessened if too many sets are performed. A recommended program for beginners in their first year of training is three heavy sets (up to the maximum number of repetitions) preceded by one or two light warm-up sets using about 50 percent of the 1 RM.

To make the exercise program more time-effective, two or three exercises that require different muscle groups may be alternated. In this manner, an individual will not have to wait the full ninety seconds before proceeding to the next set. For example, bench press, leg extension, and sit-up exercises may be combined so that the person can go almost directly from one set to the next.

Additionally, to avoid muscle soreness and stiffness, new participants ought to build up gradually to the three sets of maximal repetitions. This can be accomplished by only doing one set of each exercise with a lighter resistance on the first day. During the second session, two sets of each exercise can be performed — one light and the second with the regular resistance. For the third session, three sets could be performed — one light and two heavy ones. Thereafter, a person should be able to do all three heavy sets.

Frequency of Training

Strength training should be done either with a total body workout three times per week, or more frequently if a split-body routine (upper body one day and lower body the next) is used. Following a maximum workout, it is necessary to rest the muscles for about forty-eight hours to allow adequate recovery. If complete recovery has not occurred in two or three days, the person is most likely overtraining and therefore not reaping the full benefits of the program. In such a case, a decrease in the total number of sets and/or exercises performed on the previous workout is recommended.

To achieve significant strength gains, a minimum of eight weeks of consecutive training is needed. Once an ideal level of strength is achieved, one training session per week will be sufficient to maintain the new strength level.

Designing Your Own Strength-Training Program

Two strength-training programs are illustrated at the end of this chapter. These programs have been developed to provide a complete body workout. Only a minimum of equipment is required for the first program, "Strength-Training Exercises Without Weights" (exercises 1 through 10). This program can be conducted within the walls of your own home. Your body weight is used as the primary resistance for most exercises. In a few instances, a friend's help or some basic implements from around your home are used to provide greater resistance. The second program, "Strength-Training Exercises With Weights" (exercises 11 through 17), requires the use of gym machines such as those shown in the various photographs. Most of these exercises can also be performed with free weights.

Depending on the facilities available to you, choose one of the two training programs illustrated at the end of this chapter. The resistance and the number of repetitions that you use should be based on whether you want to increase muscular strength or muscular endurance. Up to ten repetitions maximum should be used for strength gains and more than ten (ten to thirty) for muscular endurance. As pointed out earlier, three training sessions per week conducted on nonconsecutive days is ideal for proper development. Since both strength and endurance are required in daily activities, three to five sets of about ten repetitions maximum for each exercise are recommended. In this manner you will obtain good strength gains and yet be close to the endurance threshold as well.

Perhaps the only exercises where more than ten repetitions are recommended are the abdominal exercises. The abdominal muscles are considered primarily antigravity or postural muscles; hence, a little more endurance may be required. Most people perform about twenty repetitions when doing abdominal work. Once you initiate your strength-training program, you may use the form provided in Figure 3.11 to keep a record of your training sessions.

MUSCULAR FLEXIBILITY

Flexibility has been defined as the ability of a joint to move freely through a full range of motion. Improving and maintaining good joint range of motion throughout life is an important factor in the enhancement of health and quality of life. Flexibility fitness, nevertheless, has been generally underestimated and overlooked by health care professionals and practitioners.

The degree of flexibility possessed by an individual seems to be determined by heredity and exercise. Joint range of motion is limited by factors such as joint structure, ligaments, tendons, muscles, skin, tissue injury, adipose tissue, body temperature, age, gender, and index of physical activity.

On the average, women enjoy higher flexibility levels than men and seem to retain this advantage throughout life. Aging also decreases the extensibility of soft tissue, resulting in decreased flexibility. The most significant contributors to decrements in flexibility, however, are sedentary living and lack of physical activity. As physical activity decreases, muscles lose elasticity, and tendons and ligaments tighten and shorten.

Mild stretching exercises in conjunction with calisthenics are helpful in warm-up routines to prepare the body for more vigorous aerobic or strength-training exercises, as well as subsequent cool-down routines to help the body return to the normal resting state. Generally, flexibility exercises to improve joint range of motion are conducted following an aerobic workout. Stretching exercises seem to be most effective when a person is properly warmed up. Changes in muscle temperature can increase or decrease flexibility by as much as 20 percent. Cool temperatures have the opposite effect, decreasing joint range of motion. Because of the effects of temperature on muscular flexibility, many people prefer to conduct their stretching exercises following the aerobic phase of their workout.

Muscular Flexibility Prescription

The overload and specificity of training principles also apply to the development of muscular flexibility. To increase the total range of motion of a given joint, the specific muscles that surround that particular joint have to be progressively stretched beyond their normal accustomed length. Principles of mode, intensity, repetitions, and frequency of exercise can also be used for the prescription of flexibility programs.

Mode of Exercise

Three modes of stretching exercises can be used to increase flexibility: (a) ballistic stretching, (b) slow-sustained stretching, and (c) proprioceptive neuromuscular facilitation stretching. Although research has indicated that all three modes are effective in developing joint range of motion, ballistic stretching is no longer used in flexibility fitness programs.

Ballistic or dynamic stretching exercises are performed using jerky, rapid, and bouncy movements that provide the necessary force to lengthen the muscles. Ballistic actions, however, may lead to increased muscle soreness and injury due to small tears to the soft tissue. If the magnitude of the stretching force cannot be adequately controlled, as in fast, jerky movements, ligaments can also be easily overstretched. This, in turn, leads to excessively loose joints, increasing the risk for injuries, including joint dislocation and subluxation (partial dislocation). Consequently, most authorities do not recommend ballistic exercises for flexibility development.

With the slow-sustained stretching technique, muscles are gradually lengthened through a joint's complete range of motion, and the final position is held for ten to sixty seconds. Using a slow-sustained stretch causes the muscles to relax; hence, greater length can be achieved. This type of stretch causes relatively little pain and has a very low risk of injury. Slow-sustained stretching exercises are the most frequently used and recommended for flexibility development programs.

Proprioceptive neuromuscular facilitation (PNF) stretching has become more popular in the last few years. This technique is based on a "contract and relax" method and requires the assistance of another person. The procedure used is as follows:

A. The person assisting with the exercise provides an initial force by slowly pushing in the direction of the desired stretch. The initial stretch does not cover the entire range of motion.

B. The person being stretched then applies force in the opposite direction of the stretch, against the assistant, who will try to hold the initial degree of stretch as closely as possible. In other words, an isometric contraction is being performed at that angle.

C. After four or five seconds of isometric contraction, the muscle(s) being stretched are completely relaxed. The assistant then slowly increases the degree of stretch to a greater angle.

D. The isometric contraction is then repeated for another four or five seconds, following which the muscle(s) is relaxed again. The assistant can then slowly increase the degree of stretch one more time. This procedure is repeated anywhere from two to five times until mild discomfort occurs. On the last trial, the final stretched position should be held for ten to sixty seconds.

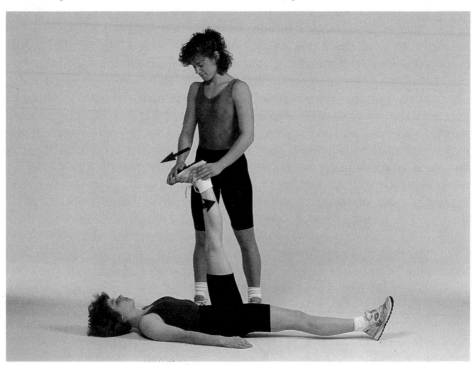

FIGURE 3.6. Proprioceptive neuromuscular facilitation stretching technique.

Theoretically, with the PNF technique, the isometric contraction aids in the relaxation of the muscle(s) being stretched, which results in greater muscle length. While some researchers have indicated that PNF is more effective than slow-sustained stretching, the disadvantages are that the degree of pain incurred with PNF is greater, a second person is required to perform the exercises, and a greater period of time is needed to conduct each session.

Intensity of Exercise

Before starting any flexibility exercises, always warm up the muscles adequately with some calisthenic exercises. As has been mentioned earlier, a good time to do flexibility exercises is following aerobic workouts. Increased body temperature can significantly increase joint range of motion. Failing to conduct a proper warm-up increases the risk for muscle pulls and tears.

The intensity or degree of stretch when doing flexibility exercises should only be to a point of mild discomfort. Pain does not have to be a part of the stretching routine. Excessive pain is an indication that the load is too high and may lead to injury. Stretching should only be done to slightly below the pain threshold. As you reach this point, you should try to relax the muscle(s) being stretched as much as possible. After completing the stretch, bring the body part gradually back to the original starting point.

Repetitions

The duration of an exercise session for flexibility development is based on the repetitions performed for each exercise and the length of time that each repetition (final stretched position) is held. The general recommendations are that each exercise be done four or five times, and each time the final position should be held for about ten seconds. As the flexibility levels increase, the subject can progressively increase the time that each repetition is held, up to a maximum of one minute.

Frequency of Exercise

Flexibility exercises should be conducted five to six times per week in the initial stages of the program. After a minimum of six to eight weeks of almost daily stretching, flexibility levels can be maintained with only two or three sessions per week, using about three repetitions of ten to fifteen seconds each.

Designing a Flexibility Program

To improve overall body flexibility, at least one stretching exercise should be used for each major muscle group. A complete set of exercises for the development of muscular flexibility is given at the end of this chapter. For some of these exercises (e.g., lateral head tilts and arm circles) you may not be able to hold a final stretched position, but you should still perform the exercise through the joint's full range of motion.

Depending on the number and the length of the repetitions performed, a complete workout will last between fifteen and sixty minutes.

PREVENTION AND REHABILITATION OF LOW BACK PAIN

Very few people make it through life without suffering from low back pain at some point. Current estimates indicate that 75 million Americans suffer from chronic low back pain each year. Unfortunately, approximately 80 percent of the time, backache syndrome is preventable and is caused by: (a) physical inactivity, (b) poor postural habits and body mechanics, and/or (c) excessive body weight.

Lack of physical activity is the most common cause contributing to chronic low back pain. The deterioration or weakening of the abdominal and gluteal muscles, along with a tightening of the lower back (erector spine) muscles, bring about an unnatural forward tilt of the pelvis (see Figure 3.7). This tilt puts extra pressure on the spinal vertebrae, causing pain in the lower back. In addition, excessive accumulation of fat around the midsection of the body contributes to the forward tilt of the pelvis, which further aggravates the condition.

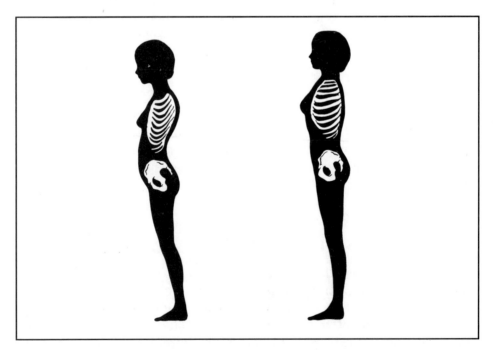

FIGURE 3.7. Incorrect (left) and correct (right) pelvic alignment.

Low back pain is also frequently associated with faulty posture and improper body mechanics. This refers to the use of correct body positions in all of life's daily activities, including sleeping, sitting, standing, walking, driving, working, and exercising. Incorrect posture and poor mechanics, as explained in Figure 3.8, lead to increased strain not only on the lower back, but on many other bones, joints, muscles, and ligaments.

The incidence and frequency of low back pain can be greatly reduced by including some specific stretching and strengthening exercises in your regular fitness program. When suffering from backache, in most cases pain is only present with movement and physical activity. If the pain is severe and persists even at rest, the initial step is to consult a physician, who can rule out any disc damage and most likely prescribe correct bed rest using several pillows under the knees for adequate leg support (see Figure 3.8). This position helps relieve muscle spasms by stretching the muscles involved. Additionally, a physician may prescribe a muscle relaxant, and/or anti-inflammatory medication, and/or some type of physical therapy. Once the individual is pain-free in the resting state, he/she needs to start correcting the muscular imbalance by stretching the tight muscles and strengthening weak ones (stretching exercises are always performed first). Because of the significance of these exercises in the prevention and rehabilitation of the backache syndrome, the exercises have also been included at the end of this chapter. You should conduct these exercises twice or more daily when suffering from back ache. Under normal conditions, three to four times per week is sufficient to prevent the syndrome.

TIPS TO ENHANCE EXERCISE ADHERENCE

Different things motivate different people to join and remain in a fitness program. Regardless of what the initial reason was for initiating an exercise program, you now need to plan for ways to make your workout fun. The psychology behind it is simple. If you enjoy an activity, you will continue to do it. If you don't, you will quit. Some of the following suggestions may help:

1. Select aerobic activities that you enjoy doing. Picking an activity that you don't enjoy decreases your chances for exercise adherence.

2. Use a combination of different activities. You can train by using two or three different activities during the same week. For some people this decreases the monotony of repeating the same activity every day.

Your Back and How to Care For It

HOW TO STAY ON YOUR FEET WITHOUT TIRING YOUR BACK

To prevent strain and pain in everyday activities, it is restful to change from one task to another before fatigue sets in. Housewives can lie down between chores, others should check body position frequently, drawing in the abdomen, flattening the back, bending the knees slightly.

Not this way — **Use of a footrest relieves swayback.**

Not this way — **Bend the knees and hips, not the waist.**

Not this way — **Hold heavy objects close to you.**

Not this way — **Never bend over without bending the knees.**

HOW TO PUT YOUR BACK TO BED

For proper bed posture, a firm mattress is essential. Bedboards, sold commercially, or devised at home, may be used with soft mattresses. Bedboards, preferably, should be made of ¾ inch plywood. Faulty sleeping positions intensify swayback and result not only in backache but in numbness, tingling, and pain in arms and legs.

Incorrect: Lying flat on back makes swayback worse

Correct: Lying on side with knees bent effectively flattens the back. Flat pillow may be used to support neck, especially when shoulders are broad.

Use of high pillow strains neck, arms, shoulders

Sleeping on back is restful and correct when knees are properly supported.

Sleeping face down exaggerates swayback, strains neck and shoulders

Raise the foot of the mattress eight inches to discourage sleeping on the abdomen.

Bending one hip and knee does not relieve swayback

Proper arrangement of pillows for resting or reading in bed.

HOW TO SIT CORRECTLY

A back's best friend is a straight, hard chair. If you can't get the chair you prefer, learn to sit properly on whatever chair you get. To correct sitting position from forward slump: Throw head well back, then bend it forward to pull in the chin. This will straighten the back. Now tighten abdominal muscles to raise the chest. Check position frequently.

Relieve strain by sitting well forward, flatten back by tightening abdominal muscles, and cross knees.

Use of footrest relieves swayback. Aim is to have knees higher than hips.

Correct way to sit while driving, close to pedals. Use seat belt or hard backrest, available commercially.

TV slump leads to "dowager's hump," strains neck and shoulders.

If chair is too high, swayback is increased.

Keep neck and back in as straight a line as possible with the spine. Bend forward from hips.

Driver's seat too far from pedals emphasizes curve in lower back.

Strained reading position. Forward thrusting strains muscles of neck and head.

Reproduced with permission of Schering Corporation. Copyright Schering Corporation, Kenilworth, NJ.

FIGURE 3.8.

3. Have a friend work out with you. The social interaction will make exercise more fulfilling. Besides, it's harder to skip if someone else is waiting for you.

4. Set aside a regular time for exercise. If you don't plan ahead, it is a lot easier to skip. Holding your exercise hour "sacred" helps you adhere to the program.

5. Obtain adequate equipment for exercise. A poor pair of shoes, for example, can increase the risk for injury, leading to discouragement right from the beginning.

6. Don't become a chronic exerciser. Learn to listen to your body. Overexercising can lead to chronic fatigue and injuries. Exercise should be enjoyable, and in the process you will need to "stop and smell the roses."

7. Exercise in different places and facilities (if feasible). This practice will add variety to your workouts.

8. Conduct periodic assessments. Improving to a higher fitness category is fun and a reward by itself.

9. Keep a regular record of your activities. In this manner, you will be able to monitor your progress and compare with previous months and years. You can use forms similar to those in Figures 3.11 and 3.12 to monitor your aerobic and strength-training programs respectively.

10. See a physician when health problems arise. When in doubt, "it is better to be safe than sorry."

11. Set realistic fitness goals to provide direction to your program. Reward yourself when you accomplish a certain goal (e.g., improving to a higher level of cardiovascular endurance, reaching a certain percent body fat). Buy new clothing, a tennis racquet, a bicycle, exercise shoes, or something else that is special and would have not been acquired otherwise.

SETTING FITNESS GOALS

Before you leave this chapter, it is imperative that you consider your fitness goals. In the last few decades we have become accustomed to "quick fixes" with everything from fast foods to one hour dry cleaning. There is, however, no "quick fix" for fitness. Fitness takes time and dedication to develop and only those who are committed and persistent will reap the rewards. In this regard, setting realistic fitness goals will help you design and provide guidance to your program. Figure 3.9 contains a goal-setting chart that will help you determine your fitness goals. You are encouraged to take the time, either by yourself or with the help of your instructor, and fill it out.

As you prepare to write realistic fitness goals, you should do so based on the results of your initial fitness tests (pre-test). For instance, if your cardiovascular fitness category was poor on the pre-test, it would be unrealistic to expect to improve to the excellent category in a little over three months. Additionally, and whenever possible, your goals should be measurable. A goal that simply states "to improve cardiovascular endurance" is not as measurable as goal that states "to improve to the good fitness category in cardiovascular endurance" or "to run the 1.5-mile course in eleven minutes or less." After determining each goal, you will also need to write measurable objectives to accomplish that goal. These objectives will be your actual plan of attack to accomplish the goal. A sample of objectives to accomplish the previously stated goal for cardio-vascular endurance development could be: (1) I will use jogging as my mode of exercise; (2) I will jog at 10:00 a.m. five times per week; (3) I will jog around the track in the fieldhouse; (4) I will jog for thirty minutes each time that I exercise; (5) I will monitor my heart rate regularly while I exercise; and (6) I will take the 1.5-mile run test once a month.

Keep in mind that there will be times when specific objectives are not being met. Consequently, your goal may be out of reach. In such cases you will need to reevaluate your objectives and make adjustments accordingly. If you set unrealistic goals at the beginning of your exercise program, be flexible with yourself and reconsider your plan of action, but do not quit. Reconsidering your plan of action does not mean failure. Failure only comes to those that stop trying, while success will come to those who are committed and persistent.

Indicate below two or three general goals that you will work on during the next few weeks and write the specific objectives that you will use to accomplish each goal (you may not need eight specific objectives, only write as many as you need).

Cardiovascular Endurance Goal: _____

Specific Objectives:

1. ~~To run 6 miles regularily~~. 0/18
2. ~~aerobics twice a week~~
3. ride bike 3 x week
4. _____
5. _____
6. _____
7. _____
8. _____

Muscular Strength/Endurance Goal: _____

Specific Objectives:

1. ~~Strengthen upper body more~~
2. ~~weightlift 3 x a week~~
3. work on my upper body strength
4. tone up my legs
5. _____
6. _____
7. _____
8. _____

(Continued)

FIGURE 3.9. Goal setting chart.

Muscular Flexibility Goal: _____

Specific Objectives:

1. _Stretch out more offta before activities!_
2. _____
3. _____
4. _____
5. _____
6. _____
7. _____
8. _____

Body Composition Goal: _____

Specific Objectives:

1. _Less % of fat, maybe - I'm at 17.5%_
2. _____
3. _____
4. _____
5. _____
6. _____
7. _____
8. _____

FIGURE 3.9. Goal setting chart. (continued)

Name _____ Month _____

Date	Body Weight	Exercise Heart Rate	Type of Exercise	Distance In Miles	Time Hrs./Min.
1					
2					
3					
4					
5					
6					
7				*10/17*	
8					
9					
10					
11					
12	-118		Karate/run	1 mile	
13		H/ 23	running	2½ miles	17/10 min
14			running again	1½ mile	
15					
16					
17					
18					
19					
20					
21					
22					
23					
24					
25					
26					
27					
28					
29					
30					
31					
			Total		

FIGURE 3.10. Aerobics record form.

Fitness and Wellness

Name _____ Month _____

Date	Body Weight	Exercise Heart Rate	Type of Exercise	Distance In Miles	Time Hrs./Min.
1					
2					
3					
4					
5					
6					
7					
8					
9					
10					
11					
12					
13					
14					
15					
16					
17					
18					
19					
20					
21					
22					
23					
24					
25					
26					
27					
28					
29					
30					
31					
			Total		

FIGURE 3.10. Aerobics record form (continued).

Name _____ Month _February_

Date	Body Weight	Exercise Heart Rate	Type of Exercise	Distance In Miles	Time Hrs./Min.
1					
2					
3					
4					
5					
6					
7					
8					
9					
10					
11	130	30	walking aerobic		20 min.
12	130	28	walked	~1.25	25
13	''	27	weights	—	15
14	''	28	walked	~1	20
15	''	26	weights	—	15
16					
17					
18	''	28	weights	—	15
19	''	27	walked	~1	20
20					
21	''	28	weights	—	15
22	''	28	walked	~1	25
23					
24	''	27	weights	—	10
25	''	29	walked	~1	25
26	''	27	weights	—	20
27	''	28	walked	~1	15
28					
29	''	27	weights	—	20
30					
31					
			Total		

FIGURE 3.10. Aerobics record form (continued).

Name _____ Month _____

Date	Body Weight	Exercise Heart Rate	Type of Exercise	Distance In Miles	Time Hrs./Min.
1	130	30	walked	~1	20
2					
3					
4	''	27	weights	⊂——	20
5	''	29	walked	~1.25	25
6	''		walked	~1	15
7					
8	''	29	walked	~1	15
9	128	26	weights	⊂——	15
10					
11					
12	''	27	walked	~1	20
13					
14	129	27	walked	~1.25	25
15					
16					
17					
18					
19					
20					
21					
22					
23					
24					
25					
26					
27					
28					
29					
30					
31					
			Total		

FIGURE 3.10. Aerobics record form (continued).

Name _____

Date									
Exercise	St/Reps/Res*	St/Reps/Res*	St/Reps/Res*	St/Reps/Res*	St/Reps/Res*	St/Reps/Res*	St/Reps/Res*	St/Reps/Res*	St/Reps/Res*

*St/Reps/Res = Sets, Repetitions, and Resistance (e.g., 1/6/125 = 1 set of 6 repetitions with 125 pounds).

FIGURE 3.11. Strength training record form.

Name _____

Date	Exercise	St/Reps/Res*	St/Reps/Res*	St/Reps/Res*	St/Reps/Res*	St/Reps/Res*	St/Reps/Res*	St/Reps/Res*	St/Reps/Res*	St/Reps/Res*

*St/Reps/Res = Sets, Repetitions, and Resistance (e.g., 1/6/125 = 1 set of 6 repetitions with 125 pounds).

FIGURE 3.11. Strength training record form (continued).

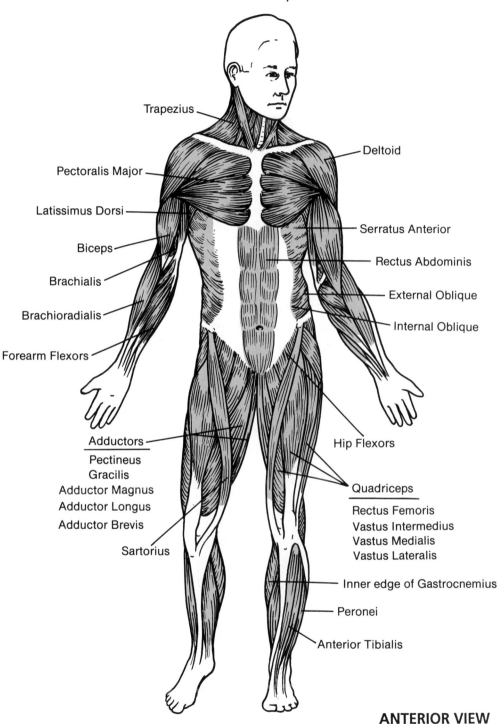

Trapezius

Deltoid

Pectoralis Major

Latissimus Dorsi

Serratus Anterior

Biceps

Rectus Abdominis

Brachialis

External Oblique

Brachioradialis

Internal Oblique

Forearm Flexors

Adductors

Hip Flexors

Pectineus
Gracilis
Adductor Magnus
Adductor Longus
Adductor Brevis

Quadriceps

Rectus Femoris
Vastus Intermedius
Vastus Medialis
Vastus Lateralis

Sartorius

Inner edge of Gastrocnemius

Peronei

Anterior Tibialis

ANTERIOR VIEW

FIGURE 3.12. Major muscles of the human body (anterior view).

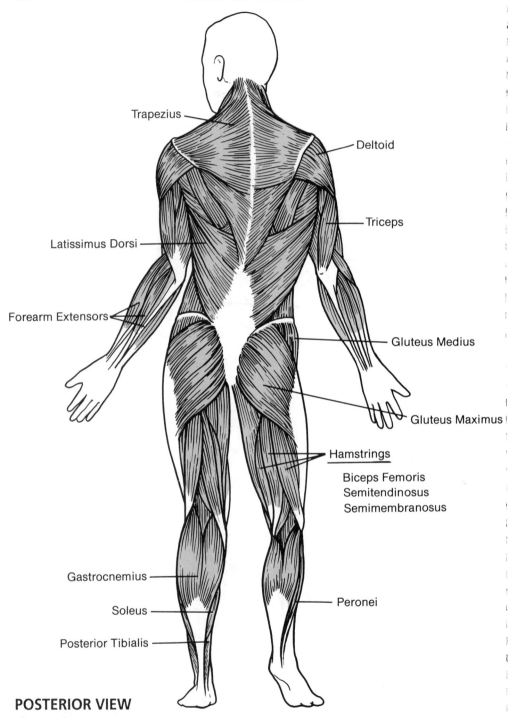

POSTERIOR VIEW

FIGURE 3.12. Major muscles of the human body (posterior view).

EXERCISES

- **Strength-Training Exercises Without Weights**
- **Strength-Training Exercises With Weights***
- **Flexibility Exercises**
- **Exercises for the Prevention and Rehabilitation of Low Back Pain**

---

*Photographs for Exercises 11, 13, 16, and 17 are courtesy of Universal Gym® Equipment, Inc., 930 27th Avenue, S.W., Cedar Rapids, IA 52406. Photographs for Exercises 12, 14, and 15 are courtesy of Nautilus®, a registered trademark of Nautilus® Sports/Medical Industries, Inc., P.O. Box 809014, Dallas, TX 75380-9014.

STRENGTH-TRAINING EXERCISES WITHOUT WEIGHTS

EXERCISE **1**

Step-Up

a

Action: Step up and down using a box or chair approximately twelve to fifteen inches high. Conduct one set using the same leg each time you go up and then conduct a second set using the other leg. You could also alternate legs on each step-up cycle. You may increase the resistance by holding a child or some other object in your arms (hold the child or object close to the body to avoid increased strain in the lower back).

Muscles Developed: Gluteal muscles, quadriceps, gastrocnemius, and soleus.

b

c

EXERCISE **2**

High-Jumper

Action: Start with the knees bent at approximately 150° and jump as high as you can, raising both arms simultaneously.

Muscles Developed: Gluteal muscles, quadriceps, gastrocnemius, and soleus.

a

b

EXERCISE 3

Push-Up

a

b

c

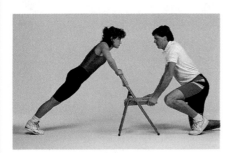

d

e

Action: Maintaining your body as straight as possible, flex the elbows, lowering the body until you almost touch the floor, then raise yourself back up to the starting position. If you are unable to perform the push-up as indicated, you can decrease the resistance by supporting the lower body with the knees rather than the feet (see illustration c) or using an incline plane and supporting your hands at a higher point than the floor (see illustration d). If you wish to increase the resistance, have someone else add resistance to your shoulders as you are coming back up (see illustration e).

Muscles Developed: Triceps, deltoid, pectoralis major, erector spinae, and abdominals.

EXERCISE **4**

Abdominal Curl-Up and Abdominal Crunch

Action: Start with your head and shoulders off the floor, arms crossed on your chest, and knees slightly bent (the greater the flexion of the knee, the more difficult the sit-up). Now curl up to about 30° (abdominal crunch — see illustration b) or curl all the way up (abdominal curl-up), then return to the starting position without letting the head or shoulders touch the floor, or allowing the hips to come off the floor. If you allow the hips to raise off the floor and the head and shoulders to touch the floor (see illustration d), you will most likely "swing up" on the next sit-up, which minimizes the work of the abdominal muscles. If you cannot curl up with the arms on the chest, place the hands by the side of the hips or even help yourself up by holding on to your thighs (illustrations e and f). Do not perform the sit-up exercise with your legs completely extended, as this will cause strain on the lower back.

Muscles Developed: Abdominal muscles and hip flexors.

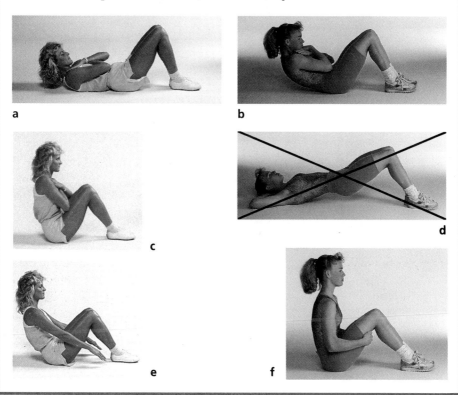

a

b

c

d

e

f

EXERCISE 5

Leg Curl

Action: Lie on the floor face down. Cross the right ankle over the left heel. Apply resistance with your right foot, while you bring the left foot up to 90° at the knee joint. (Apply enough resistance so that the left foot can only be brought up slowly.) Repeat the exercise, crossing the left ankle over the right heel.

Muscles Developed: Hamstrings (and quadriceps).

a

b

EXERCISE **6**

Modified Dip

Action: Place your hands and feet on opposite chairs with knees slightly bent (make sure that the chairs are well stabilized). Dip down at least to a 90° angle at the elbow joint, then return to the initial position. To increase the resistance, have someone else hold you down by the shoulders on the way up (see illustration c).

Muscles Developed: Triceps, deltoid, and pectoralis major.

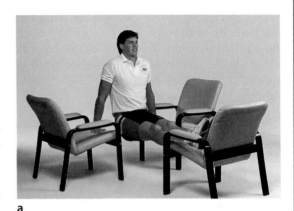

a

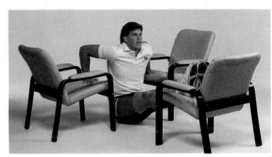

b

c

EXERCISE **7**

Pull-Up

Action: Suspend yourself from a bar with a pronated grip (thumbs in). Pull you body up until your chin is above the bar, then lower the body slowly to the starting position. If you are unable to perform the pull-up as described, either have a partner hold your feet to push off and facilitate the movement upward (illustrations c and d) or use a lower bar and support your feet on the floor (illustration e).

Muscles Developed:
Biceps, brachio-radialis, brachialis, trapezius, and latissimus dorsi.

a

b

c

d

e

EXERCISE **8**

Arm Curl

Action: Using a palms-up grip, start with the arm completely extended, and with the aid of a sandbag or bucket filled (as needed) with sand or rocks, curl up as far as possible, then return to the initial position. Repeat the exercise with the other arm.

Muscles Developed: Biceps, brachioradialis, and brachialis.

a   b

EXERCISE 9

Heel Raise

Action: From a standing position with feet flat on the floor, raise and lower your body weight by moving at the ankle joint only (for added resistance, have someone else hold your shoulders down as you perform the exercise).

Muscles Developed: Gastrocnemius and soleus.

a

b

_____ EXERCISE **10** _____

Leg Abduction and Adduction

Action: Both participants sit on the floor. The subject on the left places the feet on the inside of the other participant's feet. Simultaneously, the subject on the left presses the legs laterally (to the outside — abduction), while the subject on the right presses the legs medially (adduction). Hold the contraction for five to ten seconds. Repeat the exercise at all three angles, and then reverse the pressing sequence. The subject on the left places the feet on the outside and presses inward, while the subject on the right presses outward.

Muscles Developed: Hip abductors (rectus femoris, sartori, gluteus medius and minimus), and adductors (pectineus, gracilis, adductor magnus, adductor longus, and adductor brevis).

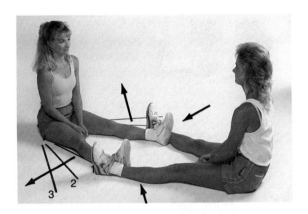

STRENGTH-TRAINING EXERCISES WITH WEIGHTS

EXERCISE **11**

a

Arm Curl

Action: Use a supinated or palms-up grip, and start with the arms almost completely extended. Now curl up as far as possible, then return to the starting position.

Muscles Developed: Biceps, brachioradialis, and brachialis.

b

EXERCISE **12**

Bench Press

Action: Lie down on the bench with the head by the weight stack, the bench press bar above the chest, and keep the feet on the floor. Grasp the bar handles and press upward until the arms are completely extended, then return to the original position. Do not arch the back during this exercise.

Muscles Developed: Pectoralis major, triceps, and deltoid.

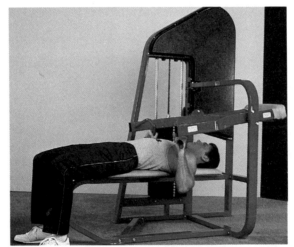

a

b

EXERCISE **13**

Sit-Up

Action: Using either a horizontal or an inclined board, stabilize your feet and flex the knees to about 100 to 120 degrees. Start with the head and shoulders off the board, curl all the way up, then return to the starting position without letting the head and shoulder touch the board (do not swing up, but rather curl up). You may curl straight up or use a twisting motion (twisting as you first start to come up), alternating on each sit-up.

Muscles Developed: Abdominals and hip flexors.

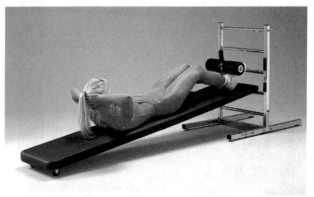

a

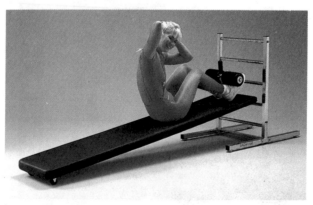

b

EXERCISE **14**

Leg Extension

Action: Sit in an upright position with the feet under the padded bar and grasp the handles at the sides. Extend the legs until they are completely straight, then return to the starting position.

Muscles Developed: Quadriceps.

a

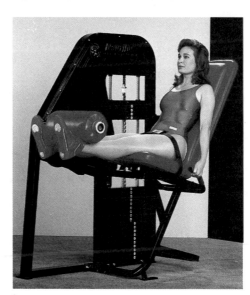

b

EXERCISE **15**

Leg Curl

Action: Lie with the face down on the bench, legs straight, and place the back of the feet under the padded bar. Curl up to at least 90°, and return to the original position.

Muscles Developed: Hamstrings.

a

b

EXERCISE **16**

Lateral Pull-Down

Action: Start from a sitting position, and hold the exercise bar with a wide grip. Pull the bar down until it touches the base of the neck, then return to the starting position (if a heavy resistance is used, stabilization of the body may be required by either using equipment as shown or by having someone else hold you down by the waist or shoulders).

Muscles Developed: Latissimus dorsi, pectoralis major, and biceps.

a   b

EXERCISE **17**

Heel Raise

Action: Start with your feet either flat on the floor or the front of the feet on an elevated block, then raise and lower yourself by moving at the ankle joint only. If additional resistance is needed, you can use a squat strength-training machine.

Muscles Developed: Gastrocnemius and soleus.

a

b

FLEXIBILITY EXERCISES

EXERCISE **18**

Lateral Head Tilt

Action: Slowly and gently tilt the head laterally. Repeat several times to each side.

Areas Stretched: Neck flexors and extensors and ligaments of the cervical spine.

EXERCISE **19**

Arm Circles

Action: Gently circle your arms all the way around. Conduct the exercise in both directions.

Areas Stretched: Shoulder muscles and ligaments.

EXERCISE 20

Side Stretch

Action: Stand straight up, feet separated to shoulder width, and place your hands on your waist. Now move the upper body to one side and hold the final stretch for a few seconds. Repeat on the other side.

Areas Stretched: Muscles and ligaments in the pelvic region.

—— EXERCISE **21** ——

Body Rotation

Action: Place your arms slightly away from your body and rotate the trunk as far as possible, holding the final position for several seconds. Conduct the exercise for both the right and left sides of the body. You can also perform this exercise by standing about two feet away from the wall (back toward the wall), and then rotate the trunk, placing the hands against the wall.

Areas Stretched: Hip, abdominal, chest, back, neck, and shoulder muscles; hip and spinal ligaments.

EXERCISE **22**

Chest Stretch

Action: Kneel down behind a chair and place both hands on the back of the chair. Gradually push your chest downward and hold for a few seconds.

Areas Stretched: Chest (pectoral) muscles and shoulder ligaments.

EXERCISE 23

Shoulder Hyperextension Stretch

Action: Have a partner grasp your arms from behind by the wrists and slowly push them upward. Hold the final position for a few seconds.

Areas Stretched: Deltoid and pectoral muscles, and ligaments of the shoulder joint.

EXERCISE 24

Shoulder Rotation Stretch

Action: With the aid of surgical tubing or an aluminum or wood stick, place the tubing or stick behind your back and grasp the two ends using a reverse (thumbs-out) grip. Slowly bring the tubing or stick over your head, keeping the elbows straight. Repeat several times (bring the hands closer together for additional stretch).

Areas Stretched: Deltoid, latissimus dorsi, and pectoral muscles; shoulder ligaments.

EXERCISE 25

Quad Stretch

Action: Stand straight up and bring up one foot, flexing the knee. Grasp the front of the ankle and pull the ankle toward the gluteal region. Hold for several seconds. Repeat with the other leg.

Areas Stretched: Quadriceps muscle, and knee and ankle ligaments.

Heel Cord Stretch

Action: Stand against the wall or at the edge of a step and stretch the heel downward, alternating legs. Hold the stretched position for a few seconds.

Areas Stretched: Heel cord (Achilles tendon), gastrocnemius, and soleus muscles.

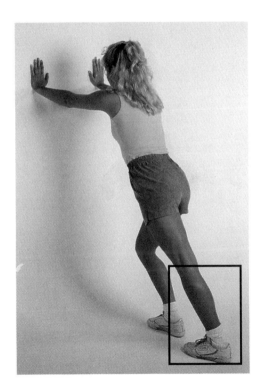

EXERCISE **27**

Adductor Stretch

Action: Stand with your feet about twice shoulder width and place your hands slightly above the knee. Flex one knee and slowly go down as far as possible, holding the final position for a few seconds. Repeat with the other leg.

Areas Stretched: Hip adductor muscles.

EXERCISE **28**

Sitting Adductor Stretch

Action: Sit on the floor and bring your feet in close to you, allowing the soles of the feet to touch each other. Now place your forearms (or elbows) on the inner part of the thigh and push the legs downward, holding the final stretch for several seconds.

Areas Stretched: Hip adductor muscles.

EXERCISE **29**

Sit-and-Reach Stretch

Action: Sit on the floor with legs together and gradually reach forward as far as possible. Hold the final position for a few seconds. This exercise may also be performed with the legs separated, reaching to each side as well as to the middle.

Areas Stretched: Hamstrings and lower back muscles, and lumbar spine ligaments.

Triceps Stretch

Action: Place the right hand behind your neck. Grasp the right arm above the elbow with the left hand. Gently pull the elbow backward. Repeat the exercise with the opposite arm.

Areas Stretched: Back of upper arm (triceps muscle) and shoulder joint.

EXERCISES FOR THE PREVENTION AND REHABILITATION OF LOW BACK PAIN

EXERCISE **31**

Single-Knee to Chest Stretch

Action: Lie down flat on the floor. Bend one leg at approximately 100° and gradually pull the opposite leg toward your chest. Hold the final stretch for a few seconds. Switch legs and repeat the exercise.

Areas Stretched: Lower back and hamstring muscles, and lumbar spine ligaments.

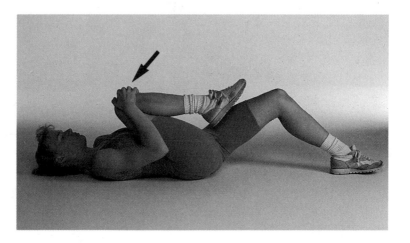

EXERCISE **32**

Double-Knee to Chest Stretch

Action: Lie flat on the floor and then slowly curl up into a fetal position. Hold for a few seconds.

Areas Stretched: Upper and lower back and hamstring muscles; spinal ligaments.

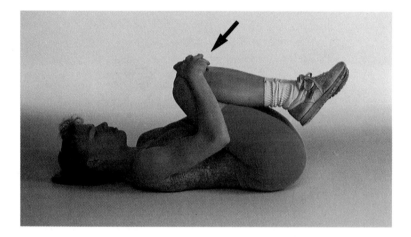

EXERCISE 33

Upper and Lower Back Stretch

Action: Sit in a chair with feet separated greater than shoulder width. Place your arms to the inside of the thighs and bring your chest down toward the floor. At the same time, attempt to reach back as far as you can with your arms.

Areas Stretched: Upper and lower back muscles and ligaments.

EXERCISE **34**

Sit-and-Reach Stretch

(see Exercise 29 in this chapter)

Side and Lower Back Stretch

Action: As illustrated in the photograph, sit on the floor with knees bent, feet to the right side, the left foot touching the right knee, and both legs flat on the floor. Place the right hand on the left knee and the left hand next to the right hand slightly above the knee. Gently pull the right shoulder toward the left knee and at the same time you may rotate the upper body counterclockwise. Switch sides and repeat the exercise (do not arch your back while performing this exercise).

Areas Stretched: Side and lower back muscles and lower back ligaments.

Note: The stretch is felt primarily when people experience low back pain due to muscle spasm or contracture.

EXERCISE **36**

Gluteal Stretch

Action: Sit on the floor, bend the right leg and place your right ankle slightly above the left knee. Grasp the left thigh with both hands and gently pull the leg toward your chest. Repeat the exercise with the opposite leg.

Areas Stretched: Buttock area (gluteal muscles).

EXERCISE **37**

Trunk Rotation
and Lower Back Stretch

Action: Sit on the floor and bend the left leg, placing the left foot on the outside of the right knee. Place the right elbow on the left knee and push against it. At the same time, try to rotate the trunk to the left (counterclockwise). Hold the final position for a few seconds. Repeat the exercise with the other side.

Areas Stretched: Lateral side of the hip and thigh; trunk, and lower back.

EXERCISE **38**

Pelvic Tilt

Action: Lie flat on the floor with the knees bent at about a 70° angle. Tilt the pelvis by tightening the abdominal muscles, flattening your back against the floor, and raising the lower gluteal area ever so slightly off the floor (see illustration b). Hold the final position for several seconds. The exercise can also be performed against a wall (as shown in illustration c).

Areas Stretched: Low back muscles and ligaments.

Areas Strengthened: Abdominal and gluteal muscles.

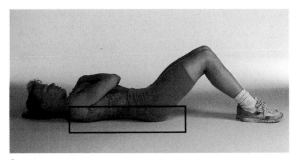

a

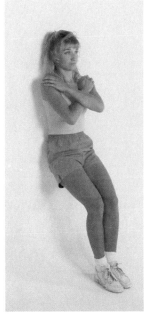

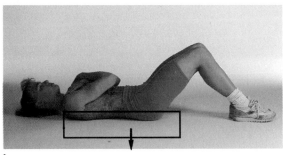

b   c

Note: This is perhaps the most important exercise for the care of the lower back. It should be included as a part of the your daily exercise routine and should be performed several times throughout the day when pain in the lower back is present as a result of muscle imbalance.

EXERCISE **39**

Abdominal Curl-Up
and Abdominal Crunch

(see Exercise 4 in this Chapter)

It is important that you do not stabilize your feet when performing either of these exercises, because doing so decreases the work of the abdominal muscles. Also, remember not to "swing up" but rather to curl up as you perform these exercises.

Nutrition and Weight Control 4

The science of nutrition studies the relationship of foods to optimal health and performance. Ample scientific evidence has long linked good nutrition to overall health and well-being. Proper nutrition signifies that a person's diet is supplying all of the essential nutrients to carry out normal tissue growth, repair, and maintenance. It also implies that the diet will provide sufficient substrates to obtain the energy necessary for work, physical activity, and relaxation.

Unfortunately, the typical American diet is too high in calories, sugars, fats, sodium, and alcohol; and too low in complex carbohydrates and fiber — none of which are conducive to good health. Over-consumption is now a major concern for many Americans.

The essential nutrients required by the human body are carbohydrates, fats, protein, vitamins, minerals, and water. Carbohydrates, fats, protein, and water are called macronutrients because large amounts are needed on a daily basis. Vitamins and minerals are only necessary in very small amounts, therefore, nutritionists commonly refer to them as micronutrients.

Depending on the amount of nutrients and calories, foods can be categorized into high nutrient density and low nutrient density. High nutrient density is used in reference to foods that contain a low or moderate amount of calories, but are packed with nutrients. Foods that are high in calories but contain few nutrients are of low nutrient density. The latter are frequently referred to as "junk food."

Carbohydrates are the major source of calories used by the body to provide energy for work, cell maintenance, and heat. They also play a

GUIDE TO GOOD EATING

Every day eat a wide variety of foods from the Four Food Groups in moderation.

Milk Group

Supplies many nutrients including:
- calcium
- protein
- riboflavin

2 servings for adults
3 servings for children
4 servings for teenagers and pregnant or breastfeeding women

Meat Group

Supplies many nutrients including:
- protein
- iron
- niacin
- thiamin

2 servings for all ages
3 servings for pregnant women

Fruit-Vegetable Group

Supplies many nutrients including:
- vitamin A
- vitamin C

4 servings for all ages

Grain Group

Supplies many nutrients including:
- carbohydrate
- iron
- thiamin
- niacin

4 servings for all ages

Combination

Foods

Combination Foods are made up of foods from more than one food group. Therefore, they supply the same nutrients as the foods they contain.

"Others"

Category

Foods in the "Others" category are often high in calories and/or low in nutrients. They don't take the place of foods from the Four Food Groups in supplying nutrients.

Condiments
Barbeque sauce
Catsup, mustard
Olives, pickles
Salt
Soy sauce

Chips and Related Products
Corn chips
Popcorn
Potato chips
Pretzels
Tortilla chips

Fats and Oils
Coffee whitener
Cream, sour cream
Gravy, cream sauce
Margarine, butter
Mayonnaise
Oil, lard, shortening
Salad dressing

Sweets
Brownies, cookies
Cakes, pies
Candy
Jelly, jam
Sugar, honey, syrup
Sweet rolls, doughnuts

Alcohol
Beer
Gin, vodka
Whiskey, rum
Wine

Other Beverages
Coffee, tea
Fruit-flavored drinks
Soft drinks

001N [1] 1989, Copyright © 1989, 5th Edition, NATIONAL DAIRY COUNCIL, Rosemont, IL 60018-4233. All rights reserved. Printed in U.S.A.

ISBN 1-55647-001-C

Guide to Good Eating courtesy of NATIONAL DAIRY COUNCIL®

FIGURE 4.1. Guide to Good Eating.

GUIDE TO GOOD EATING

Every day eat a wide variety of foods from the Four Food Groups in moderation.

You don't have to be a nutrition expert to eat for good health. The GUIDE TO GOOD EATING makes it easy. Even if you're watching your weight, looking for ways to cut back on fat or sodium, or trying to eat more fiber, this plan can work for you. Just follow the simple steps below.

Step 1—Eat foods from all Four Food Groups every day.

Foods from the Four Food Groups—Milk, Meat, Fruit-Vegetable, and Grain—can supply the more than 40 nutrients your body needs to stay healthy. Foods in each food group are good sources of different nutrients. That's why it's important to eat foods from all Four Food Groups every day.

Step 2—Include a wide variety of foods.

Foods within a food group are usually good sources of the same nutrients. But some foods are better sources of a particular nutrient than others. By eating different foods within each food group, you have a good chance of getting all the nutrients you need.

- Explore the dairy case. Try new milks, cheeses, and yogurts from the Milk Group.
- Experiment with new recipes for beef, chicken, fish, eggs, and dried beans from the Meat Group.
- Find creative ways to include foods from the Fruit-Vegetable Group. Add spinach, carrots, broccoli, mushrooms, and green pepper to your salads.
- Enjoy new tastes from the Grain Group. Try bagels, tortillas, or rye, pita, or cracked-wheat bread for sandwiches.

Step 3—Practice moderation.

By practicing moderation you can get the nutrients you need without getting too many calories or too much fat or sodium.

- Eat at least the recommended number of servings from each food group every day.
- Watch how many servings you have from the "Others" category.
- Eat foods in the serving sizes listed below.

Special Tips

If you are concerned about calories, fat, sodium, or fiber, choose foods from the Four Food Groups. Try the following:

To cut down on fat and calories:

- Begin by limiting high-fat foods from the "Others" category like salad dressings, mayonnaise, chips, cookies, cakes, and doughnuts.
- Use cooking methods that add little or no fat like baking, roasting, poaching, stir frying, steaming, and broiling.
- Choose skim, 1%, or 2% milk; lowfat or nonfat yogurt; lowfat cottage cheese; and lowfat cheeses like part-skim mozzarella.
- Select leaner cuts of meat and trim off excess fat.

To limit sodium:

- Season food with herbs and spices instead of high-sodium items like salt, soy sauce, or steak sauce.
- Choose fresh rather than canned vegetables, fish, and meats.
- Look for prepared foods that say low- or reduced-sodium on the label.

To increase fiber:

- Eat fresh fruits and vegetables with their skins.
- Select whole grain breads, bran cereals, and brown rice.
- Include dried beans and peas.

No matter what your dietary goal, it all comes down to one simple rule of thumb: *Every day eat a wide variety of foods from the Four Food Groups in moderation.*

	Serving Size	Children 1-10	Teenagers 11-18	Adults	Pregnant Women	Breastfeeding Women	Comments
				Minimum Recommended Number of Servings*			
Milk Group	Milk — 1 cup Yogurt — 1 cup Cheese — 1 oz Cottage cheese† — 1/2 cup Ice cream, ice milk, frozen yogurt† — 1/2 cup	3	4	2	4	4	†Good sources of calcium such as milk, yogurt, and cheese are recommended daily. Cottage cheese, ice cream, ice milk, and frozen yogurt have about 1/4 to 1/3 the amount of calcium per serving as milk, yogurt, and cheese.
Meat Group	Cooked, lean meat, fish, poultry — 2-3 oz Egg‡ — 1 Cooked, dried peas, dried beans‡ — 1/2 cup Peanut butter‡ — 2 tbsp Nuts, seeds‡ — 1/4 cup	2	2	2	3	2	‡Eggs, dried beans, and peanut butter have about 1/2 the amount of protein per serving as meat.
Fruit-Vegetable Group	Juice — 1/2 cup Vegetable, fruit — 1/2 cup Apple, banana, orange — 1 medium Grapefruit — 1/2 Cantaloupe — 1/4 Dried fruit — 1/4 cup	4	4	4	4	4	Dark green, leafy, or orange vegetables and fruit are recommended 3 or 4 times a week for vitamin A. Good sources of vitamin C such as oranges, strawberries, tomatoes, potatoes, and green peppers are recommended daily.
Grain Group	Bread — 1 slice English muffin, hamburger bun — 1/2 Ready-to-eat cereal — 1 oz Pasta, rice grits, cooked cereal — 1/2 cup Tortilla, roll, muffin	4	4	4	4	4	Whole grain, fortified, or enriched grain products are recommended.
Combination Foods	Soup — 1 cup Macaroni and cheese, lasagna, stew, chili, casserole — 1 cup Pizza — 1/8 15" Sandwich, taco	These count as servings (or partial servings) from the food groups from which they are made.					Combination Foods supply the same nutrients as the foods they contain.
"Others" Category	Potato chips, pretzels — 1 oz Cookies — 2 Layer cake — 1/16 9" Sugar, jelly — 1 tsp Soft drink, beer — 12 oz Margarine, butter — 1 tsp Salad dressing, mayonnaise — 1 tbsp	There is no recommended number of servings for foods in the "Others" category.					"Others" don't take the place of foods from the Four Food Groups in supplying nutrients. And they are often high in fat or calories.

*These servings provide the nutrients your body needs. They also supply about 1200 Calories. However most people need more than 1200 Calories. If you do, add more servings.

FIGURE 4.1. Guide to Good Eating (continued).

Guide to Good Eating courtesy of NATIONAL DAIRY COUNCIL®

crucial role in the digestion and regulation of fat and protein metabolism. The major sources of carbohydrates are breads, cereals, fruits, vegetables, and milk and other dairy products.

Carbohydrates are divided into simple carbohydrates and complex carbohydrates. Simple carbohydrates (such as candy, pop, and cakes) are frequently denoted as sugars and have little nutritive value. Complex carbohydrates are formed when simple carbohydrate molecules link together. Two examples of complex carbohydrates are starches and dextrins. Starches are commonly found in seeds, corn, nuts, grains, roots, potatoes, and legumes. Dextrins are formed from the breakdown of large starch molecules exposed to dry heat, such as when bread is baked or cold cereals are produced. Complex carbohydrates provide many valuable nutrients to the body and can also be an excellent source of fiber or roughage.

Dietary fiber is a type of complex carbohydrate made up of plant material that cannot be digested by the human body. It is mainly present in leaves, skins, roots, and seeds. Processing and refining foods removes almost all of the natural fiber. In our daily diets, the main sources of dietary fiber are whole-grain cereals and breads, fruits, and vegetables.

Fiber is important in the diet because it may help decrease the risk for cardiovascular disease and cancer. In addition, several other health disorders have been linked to low fiber intake, including constipation, diverticulitis, hemorrhoids, gallbladder disease, and obesity.

Fats or lipids are also used as a source of energy in the human body. They are the most concentrated source of energy. Fats are also a part of the cell structure. They are used as stored energy and as an insulator for body heat preservation. They provide shock absorption, supply essential fatty acids, and carry the fat-soluble vitamins A, D, E, and K. The basic sources of fat are milk and other dairy products, and meats and alternates.

Proteins are the main substances used to build and repair tissues such as muscles, blood, internal organs, skin, hair, nails, and bones. They are a part of hormones, enzymes, and antibodies and help maintain normal body fluid balance. Proteins can also be used as a source of energy, but only if there are not enough carbohydrates and fats available. The primary sources are meats and alternates and milk and other dairy products.

Vitamins are organic substances essential for normal metabolism, growth, and development of the body. They are classified into two types based on their solubility: fat-soluble vitamins (A, D, E, and K), and water-soluble vitamins (B complex and C). Vitamins cannot be manufactured by the body; hence, they can only be obtained through a well-balanced diet.

Minerals are inorganic elements found in the body and in food. They serve several important functions. Minerals are constituents of all cells, especially those found in hard parts of the body (bones, nails, teeth). They are crucial in the maintenance of water balance and the acid-base balance. They are essential components of respiratory pigments, enzymes, and enzyme systems, and they regulate muscular and nervous tissue excitability.

Water is the most important nutrient and is involved in almost every vital body process. Approximately 70 percent of total body weight is water. It is used in digestion and absorption of food, in the circulatory process, in removing waste products, in building and rebuilding cells, and in the transport of other nutrients. Water is contained in almost all foods but primarily in liquid foods, fruits, and vegetables. Besides the natural content in foods, it is recommended that every person drink at least eight to ten glasses of fluids a day.

A BALANCED DIET

Most people would like to live life to its fullest, maintain good health, and lead a productive life. One of the fundamental ways to accomplish this goal is by eating a well-balanced diet. Generally, daily caloric intake should be distributed in such a way that 60 percent of the total caloric intake comes from carbohydrates and less than 30 percent from fat. Saturated fats should constitute less than 10 percent of the total daily caloric intake. Protein intake should be about .8 grams per kilogram (2.2 pounds) of body weight. In addition, all of the vitamins, minerals, and water must be provided.

One of the most detrimental health habits facing the American people today is the high amount of fat in the diet. The fat consumption in the average diet is over 40 percent of the total caloric intake. If we want to enjoy better health, a deliberate effort must be made to decrease total fat intake. Therefore, being able to identify sources of fat in the diet is imperative to decrease fat intake.

Each gram of carbohydrates and protein supplies the body with four calories, while fat provides nine calories per gram consumed. In this regard, just looking at the total amount of grams consumed for each type of food can be very misleading. For example, a person who consumes 160 grams of carbohydrates, 100 grams of fat, and 70 grams of protein has a total intake of 330 grams of food. This indicates that 33 percent of the total grams of food are in the form of fat (100 grams of fat ÷ 330 grams of total food × 100). In reality, the diet consists of almost 50 percent fat calories.

In this sample diet, 640 calories are derived from carbohydrates (160 grams × 4 calories/gram), 280 calories from protein (70 grams × 4 calories/gram), and 900 calories from fat (100 grams × 9 calories/gram), for a total of 1,820 calories. If 900 calories are derived from fat, you can easily observe that almost half of the total caloric intake is in the form of fat (900 ÷ 1,820 × 100 = 49.5 percent).

Realizing that each gram of fat yields nine calories is a very useful guideline when attempting to determine the fat content of individual foods. All you need to do is multiply the grams of fat by nine and divide by the total calories in that particular food. The percentage is obtained by multiplying the latter figure by 100. For example, if a food label lists a total of 100 calories and 7 grams of fat, the fat content would be 63 percent of total calories. This simple guideline can help you decrease fat intake in your diet.

Analyzing Your Diet

Achieving and maintaining a balanced diet is not as difficult as most people think. The "Guide To Good Eating" contained in Figure 4.1 at the beginning of this chapter (published by the National Dairy Council in Rosemont, Illinois), provides simple, but sound instructions for good nutrition. The difficult part in achieving optimal nutrition, however, is retraining yourself to eat the right type of foods and avoid those that have little or no nutritive value. If you (a) avoid excessive sweets, fats, alcohol, and sodium; (b) increase your fiber intake; and (c) eat the minimum number of servings required for each one of the four basic food groups; you can achieve a well-balanced diet. The minimum number of servings of the four basic food groups for adults are (also see Figure 4.1):

A. Four or more servings per day from the grain group.

B. Four or more servings per day of fruits and vegetables, including one good source of vitamin A (apricots, cantaloupe, broccoli, carrots, pumpkin, and dark leafy green vegetables), and one good source of vitamin C (cantaloupe, citrus fruit, kiwi fruit, strawberries, broccoli, cabbage, cauliflower, and green pepper).

C. Two or more servings per day from the milk group.

D. Two or more servings per day from the meat group.

To aid you in balancing your diet, the form given in Figure 4.2 can be used to record your daily food intake. First, make as many copies of this figure as the number of days that you wish to analyze. Next, make a copy of Figure 4.1 and keep it accessible at all times. Whenever you have something to eat, record the food and the amount eaten in Figure 4.2. This information should be recorded immediately after each meal so it will be easier to keep track of your actual food intake. At the end of each day, use the list

Date: _____

Name: _*Maydawhite*_ Age: _18_   Weight: _118_ lbs.

Sex: _____ M __X__ F   (Pregnant–P, Lactating–L, Neither–N)

Activity Rating: Sedentary (limited physical activity)   = 1
                 Moderate physical activity   = (2)
                 Hard labor (strenuous physical activity) = 3

Number of days to be analyzed: _____   Day: _____ (1, 2 . . .)

No.	Code*	Food	Amount	Calories	Milk Group	Meat Group	Fruit-Vegetable Group	Grain Group
					|← Number of Servings →|			
1								
2								
3								
4								
5								
6								
7								
8								
9								
10								
11								
12								
13								
14								
15								
16								
17								
18								
19								
20								
21								
22								
23								
24								
25								
26								
27								
28								
29								
30								
Totals								
Recommended Standard				**	2	2	4	4
Deficiencies								

*See list of nutritive value of selected foods in Appendix B.
**See Table 4.1.

FIGURE 4.2. Daily diet record form.

Date: _____

Name: _____ Age: _____ Weight: _____ lbs.

Sex: _____ M _____ F (Pregnant–P, Lactating–L, Neither–N)

Activity Rating: Sedentary (limited physical activity) = 1
Moderate physical activity = 2
Hard labor (strenuous physical activity) = 3

Number of days to be analyzed: _____ Day: _____ (1, 2 . . .)

No.	Code*	Food	Amount	Calories	Milk Group	Meat Group	Fruit-Vegetable Group	Grain Group
1								
2								
3								
4								
5								
6								
7								
8								
9								
10								
11								
12								
13								
14								
15								
16								
17								
18								
19								
20								
21								
22								
23								
24								
25								
26								
27								
28								
29								
30								
Totals								
Recommended Standard				**	2	2	4	4
Deficiencies								

*See list of nutritive value of selected foods in Appendix B.
**See Table 4.1.

FIGURE 4.2. Daily diet record form (continued).

of foods contained in Appendix B at the back of this book and record the code and number of calories for all foods consumed. Also use Figure 4.1 and record the number of servings under the respective food groups. Keep in mind that if twice the amount of a standard serving is eaten, the calories and the number of servings must be doubled. You can now evaluate your diet by checking whether the minimum required servings for each food group were consumed. If you have met the required servings at the end of each day, you are doing quite well in balancing your diet.

In addition to meeting the daily servings for each of the four food groups, it is recommended that a complete nutrient analysis be conducted to accurately rate your diet. Such an analysis could pinpoint potential problem areas in your diet; such as too much fat, saturated fat, cholesterol, sodium, etc. A complete nutrient analysis can be quite an educational experience because most people do not realize how detrimental and non-nutritious many common foods are.

The process of analyzing your diet is quite simple utilizing the computer software for this analysis. Your instructor may have a copy of this software which is available through Morton Publishing Company in Englewood, Colorado. To conduct the analysis, use the information that you have already recorded on the form provided in Figure 4.2. Prior to running the software, fill out the information at the top of this form (age, weight, gender, activity rating, and number of days to be analyzed) and make sure that the foods are recorded by the code and standard amounts given in the list of selected foods contained in Appendix B. Up to seven days may be analyzed using the software. Following data entry, the computer will produce a printout with your daily totals for calories, protein, fat, saturated fat, cholesterol, carbohydrates, calcium, iron, sodium, vitamin A, thiamin, riboflavin, niacin, and vitamin C. Your printout also includes the average daily nutrient intake and the RDA (recommended dietary allowance) comparison for all of the above nutrients (see sample nutrient analysis printout in Figure 4.4 at the end of this chapter).

Vitamin and Mineral Supplementation

Another point of significant interest in nutrition is the unnecessary and sometimes unsafe use of vitamin and mineral supplementation. Even though experts agree that supplements are not necessary, people consume them at a greater rate than ever before. Research has demonstrated that even when a person consumes as few as 1,200 calories per day, no additional supplementation is needed as long as the diet contains the recommended servings from the four basic food groups.

For most people, vitamin and mineral supplementation is unnecessary. Iron deficiency (determined through blood testing) is the only exception for women who suffer from heavy menstrual flow. Pregnant and lactating women may also require supplements. In all instances, supplements should be taken under a physician's supervision. Other people that may benefit from supplementation are alcoholics who are not consuming a balanced diet, strict vegetarians, individuals on extremely low-calorie diets, elderly people who don't regularly receive balanced meals, and newborn infants (usually given a single dose of vitamin K to prevent abnormal bleeding). For healthy people with a balanced diet, supplementation provides no additional health benefits. It will not help a person run faster, jump higher, relieve stress, improve sexual prowess, cure a common cold, or boost energy levels!

Another fallacy regarding nutrition is that many people who regularly eat fast foods high in fat content and/or excessive sweets feel that vitamin and mineral supplementation is needed to balance their diet. The problem in these cases is not a lack of vitamins and minerals, but rather that the diet is too high in calories, fat, and sodium. Supplementation will not offset such poor eating habits.

EATING DISORDERS

Anorexia nervosa and bulimia have been classified as physical and emotional problems usually developed as a result of individual, family, and/or social pressures to achieve thinness. These medical disorders are steadily increasing in most industrialized nations, where low-calorie diets and model-like thinness are normal behaviors encouraged by society. Individuals who suffer from eating disorders have an intense fear of becoming obese, which does not disappear even as extreme amounts of weight are lost.

Anorexia nervosa is a condition of self-imposed starvation to lose and then maintain very low body weight. The anorexic seems to fear weight gain more than death from starvation. Furthermore, these individuals have a distorted image of their body and perceive themselves as being fat even when critically emaciated.

Although a genetic predisposition may exist, the anorexic patient often comes from a mother-dominated home, with other possible drug addictions in the family. The syndrome may start following a stressful life event and the uncertainty of the ability to cope efficiently. Because the female role in society is changing more rapidly, women seem to be especially susceptible. Life events such as weight gain, start of menstrual periods, beginning of college, loss of a boyfriend, poor self-esteem, social rejection, start of a professional career, and/or becoming a wife or mother may trigger the syndrome. The person usually begins a diet and may initially feel in control and happy about weight loss, even if not overweight. To speed up the weight loss process, severe dieting is frequently combined with exhaustive exercise and overuse of laxatives and/or diuretics. The individual commonly develops obsessive and compulsive behaviors and emphatically denies the condition. There also appears to be a constant preoccupation with food, meal planning, grocery shopping, and unusual eating habits. As weight is lost and health begins to deteriorate, the anorexic feels weak and tired and may realize that there is a problem, but will not discontinue starvation and refuses to accept the behavior as abnormal.

Once significant weight loss and malnutrition begin, typical physical changes become more visible. Some of the more common changes exhibited by anorexics are amenorrhea (cessation of menstruation), digestive difficulties, extreme sensitivity to cold, hair and skin problems, fluid and electrolyte abnormalities (which may lead to an irregular heart beat and sudden stopping of the heart), injuries to nerves and tendons, abnormalities of immune function, anemia, growth of fine body hair, mental confusion, inability to concentrate, lethargy, depression, skin dryness, and decreased skin and body temperature.

Many of the changes of anorexia nervosa are by no means irreversible. Treatment almost always requires professional help and the sooner it is started, the higher the chances for reversibility and cure. A combination of medical and psychological techniques are used in therapy to restore proper nutrition, prevent medical complications, and modify the environment or events that triggered the syndrome. Seldom are anorexics able to overcome the problem by themselves. Unfortunately, there is strong denial among anorexics and they are able to hide their condition and deceive friends and relatives quite effectively. Based on their behavior, many individuals meet all of the characteristics of anorexia nervosa, but the condition goes undetected because both thinness and dieting are socially acceptable behaviors. Only a well-trained clinician is able to make a positive diagnosis.

Bulimia, a pattern of binge eating and purging, is more prevalent than anorexia nervosa. For many years it was thought to be a variant of anorexia nervosa, but it is now identified as a separate disease.

Bulimics are usually healthy-looking people, well educated, near ideal body weight, who enjoy food and often socialize around it. However, they are emotionally insecure, rely on others, and lack self-confidence and esteem. Maintenance of ideal weight and food are both important to them. As a result of stressful life events or simple compulsion to eat, they periodically engage in binge eating that may last an hour or longer, during which several thousand calories may be consumed. A feeling of deep guilt and shame then follows, along with intense fear of gaining weight. Purging seems to be an easy answer to the problem, and the binging cycle continues without the fear of gaining weight. The most common form of purging is self-induced vomiting, although strong laxatives and emetics are frequently used. Near-fasting diets and strenuous bouts of physical activity are also commonly seen in bulimics.

Medical problems associated with bulimia include cardiac arrhythmias, amenorrhea, kidney and bladder damage, ulcers, colitis, tearing of the esophagus and/or stomach, teeth erosion, gum damage, and general muscular weakness.

Unlike anorexics, bulimics realize that their behavior is abnormal and feel great shame for their actions. Fearing social rejection, the binge-purging cycle is primarily carried out in secrecy and during unusual hours of the day. Nevertheless, bulimia can be treated successfully when the person realizes that such destructive behavior is not the solution to life's problems. Hopefully, the change in attitude will grasp the individual before permanent or fatal damage is done.

PRINCIPLES OF WEIGHT CONTROL

Achieving and maintaining ideal body weight is a major objective of a good physical fitness program. Estimates, however, indicate that only about 10 percent of all people who ever initiate a traditional weight loss program are able to lose the desired weight, and worse yet, only one in 100 is able to keep the weight off for a significant period of time. You may ask why the traditional diets have failed. The answer is simply because very few diets teach the importance of lifetime changes in food selection and the role of exercise as the keys to successful weight loss.

There are several reasons why fad diets continue to deceive people and can claim that weight will indeed be lost if "all" instructions are followed. Most diets are very low in calories and/or deprive the body of certain nutrients, creating a metabolic imbalance that can even cause death. Under such conditions, a lot of the weight loss is in the form of water and protein and not fat. On a crash diet, close to 50 percent of the weight loss is in lean (protein) tissue. When the body uses protein instead of a combination of fats and carbohydrates as a source of energy, weight is lost as much as ten times faster. A gram of protein yields half the amount of energy that fat does. In the case of muscle protein, one-fifth of protein is mixed with four-fifths water. In other words, each pound of muscle yields only one-tenth the amount of energy of a pound of fat. As a result, most of the weight loss is in the form of water, which on the scale, of course, looks good. Nevertheless, when regular eating habits are resumed, much of the lost weight comes right back.

Some diets only allow the consumption of certain foods. If people would only realize that there are no "magic" foods that will provide all of the necessary nutrients, and that a person has to eat a variety of foods to be well nourished, the diet industry would not be as successful. The unfortunate thing about most of these diets is that they create a nutritional deficiency which at times can be fatal. The reason why some of these diets succeed is because in due time people get tired of eating the same thing day in and day out and eventually start eating less. If they happen to achieve the lower weight, once they go back to old eating habits without implementing permanent dietary changes, weight is quickly gained back again.

A few diets recommend exercise along with caloric restrictions, which, of course, is the best method for weight reduction. A lot of the weight lost is due to exercise; hence, the diet has achieved its purpose. Unfortunately, if no permanent changes in food selection and activity level take place, once dieting and exercise are discontinued, the weight is quickly gained back.

Even though only a few years ago the principles that govern a weight loss and maintenance program seemed to be pretty clear, we now know that the final answers are not yet in. The traditional concepts related to weight control have been centered around three assumptions: (1) that balancing food intake against output allows a person to achieve ideal weight, (2) that fat people just eat too much, and (3) that it really does not matter to the human body how much (or little) fat is stored. While there may be some truth to these statements, they are still open to much debate and research.

Every person has a certain amount of body fat which is regulated by genetic and environmental factors. The genetic instinct to survive tells the body that fat storage is vital, and therefore it sets an inherently acceptable fat level. This level remains pretty constant or may gradually climb due to poor lifestyle habits. For instance, under strict caloric reductions, the body may make extreme metabolic adjustments in an effort to maintain its fat storage. The basal metabolic rate may drop dramatically against a consistent negative caloric balance (as in dieting), and a person may be on a plateau for days or even weeks without losing much weight. When the dieter goes back to the normal or even below normal caloric intake, at which the weight may have been stable for a long period of time, the fat loss is quickly regained as the body strives to regain a comfortable fat store.

Let's use a practical illustration. A person would like to lose some body fat and assumes that a stable body weight has been reached at an average daily caloric intake of 1,800 calories (no weight gain or loss occurs at this daily intake). This person now starts a strict low-calorie diet, or even worse, a near-fasting diet in an attempt to achieve rapid weight loss. Immediately the body activates its survival mechanism and readjusts its metabolism to a lower caloric balance. After a few weeks of dieting at less than 400 to 600 calories per day, the body can now maintain its normal functions at 1,000 calories per day. Having lost the desired weight, the person terminates the diet but realizes that the original caloric intake of 1,800 calories per day will need to be decreased to maintain the new lower weight. Therefore, to adjust to the new lower body weight, the intake is restricted to about 1,500 calories per day, but the individual is surprised to find that even at this lower daily intake (300 fewer calories), weight is gained back at a rate of one pound every one to two weeks. This new lowered metabolic rate may take a year or more after terminating the diet to kick back up to its normal level.

From this explanation, it is clear that individuals should never go on very low-calorie diets. Not only will this practice decrease resting metabolic rate, but it will also deprive the body of the basic nutrients required for normal physiological functions. Under no circumstances should a person ever engage in diets below 1,200 and 1,500 calories for women and men, respectively. Remember that weight (fat) is gained over a period of months and years and not overnight. Equally, weight loss should be accomplished gradually and not abruptly. Daily caloric intakes of 1,200 to 1,500 calories will still provide the necessary nutrients if properly distributed over the four basic food groups (meeting the daily required servings from each group). Of course, the individual will have to learn which foods meet the requirements and yet are low in fat, sugar, and calories.

Furthermore, when weight loss is pursued by means of dietary restrictions alone, there will always be a decrease in lean body mass (muscle protein, along with vital organ protein). The amount of lean body mass lost depends exclusively on the caloric restriction of your diet. In near-fasting diets, up to 50 percent of the weight loss can be lean body mass, and the other 50 percent will be actual fat loss. When diet is combined with exercise, 98 percent of the weight loss will be in the form of fat, and there may actually be an increase in lean tissue. Lean body mass loss is never desirable because it weakens the organs and muscles and slows down the metabolism.

Decreases in lean body mass are commonly seen in severely restricted diets. There are no diets with caloric intakes below 1,200 to 1,500 calories that can insure no loss of lean body mass. Even at this intake, there is some loss unless the diet is combined with exercise. Many diets have claimed that the lean component is unaltered with their particular diet, but the simple truth is that regardless of what nutrients may be added to the diet, if caloric restrictions are too severe, there will always be a loss of lean tissue.

Unfortunately, too many people constantly engage in low-calorie diets, and every time they do so, the metabolic rate keeps slowing down as more lean tissue is lost. It is not uncommon to find individuals in the forties or older who weigh the same as they did when they were twenty and feel that they are at ideal body weight. Nevertheless, during this span of twenty years or more, they have "dieted" all too many times without engaging in physical activity. The weight is regained shortly after terminating each diet, but most of that gain is in fat. Perhaps at age twenty they weighed 160 pounds and were only 15 to 16 percent fat. Now at age forty, even though they still weigh 160 pounds, they may be over 30 percent fat. They may feel that they are at ideal body weight and wonder why they are eating very little and still have a difficult time maintaining that weight.

Research has also shown that a diet high in fats and refined carbohydrates, near-fasting diets, and perhaps even artificial sweeteners will not allow a person to lose weight. On the contrary, such practices only contribute to fat gain. Therefore, it looks as though the only practical and effective way to lose fat weight is through a combination of exercise and a diet high in complex carbohydrates and low in fat and sugar.

Because of the effects of proper food management, many nutritionists now believe that the total number of calories should not be a concern in a weight control program, but rather the source of those calories. In this regard, most of the effort is spent in retraining eating habits, increasing the intake of complex carbohydrates and high-fiber foods, and decreasing the use of refined carbohydrates (sugars) and fats. In addition, a "diet" is no longer viewed as a temporary tool to aid in weight loss, but rather as a permanent change in eating behaviors to insure adequate weight management and health enhancement. The role of increased physical activity must also be considered, because successful weight loss, maintenance, and ideal body composition are seldom achieved without a regular exercise program.

Exercise: The Key to Successful Weight Management

Perhaps the most significant factor in achieving ideal body composition is a lifetime exercise program. For individuals who are trying to lose weight, a combination of an aerobic and some type of strength-training program works best. Because of the continuity and duration of aerobic activities, a large number of calories are burned during a single bout of exercise (about 400 to 600 per hour).

Strength-training exercises have the greatest impact in increasing lean body mass. Each additional pound of muscle tissue can raise the basal metabolic rate between 50 and 100 calories per day. Using the conservative estimate of 50 calories per day, an individual who adds five pounds of muscle tissue as a result of strength training would increase the basal metabolic rate by 250 calories per day, or the equivalent of 91,250 calories per year.

Since exercise leads to an increase in lean body mass, it is not uncommon for body weight to remain the same or increase when you initiate an exercise program, while inches and percent body fat decrease. The increase in lean tissue results in an increased functional capacity of the human body. With exercise, most of the weight loss is seen after a few weeks of training, when the lean component has stabilized.

It is also important to clarify that there is no such thing as spot reducing or losing "cellulite" from certain body parts. Cellulite is nothing but plain fat storage. Just doing several sets of daily sit-ups will not help to get rid of fat in the midsection of the body. When fat comes off, it does so from throughout the entire body, and not just the exercised area. The greatest proportion of fat may come off the largest fat deposits, but the caloric output of a few sets of sit-ups is practically nil to have a real effect on total body fat reduction. The amount of exercise has to be much longer to have a significant impact on weight reduction.

Dieting has never been fun and never will be. Individuals who have a weight problem and are serious about losing weight will have to make exercise a regular part of their daily life, along with proper food management, and perhaps even sensible adjustments in caloric intake. Some precautions are necessary, since excessive body fat is a risk factor for cardiovascular disease. Depending on the extent of the weight problem, a stress ECG may be required prior to initiating the exercise program. A physician should be consulted in this regard.

Significantly overweight individuals may also have to choose activities where they will not have to support their own body weight, but that will still be effective in burning calories. Joint and muscle injuries are very common among overweight individuals who participate in weight-bearing exercises such as walking, jogging, and aerobic dancing. Some better alternatives are riding a bicycle (either road or stationary), swimming, water aerobics, walking in a shallow pool, or running in place in deep water (treading water). The last three modes of exercise are quickly gaining in popularity because very little skill is required for exercise participation. These activities seem to be just as effective as other forms of aerobic activity in helping individuals lose weight without the "pain" and fear of injuries.

One final benefit of exercise related to weight control is that fat can be burned more efficiently. Since both carbohydrates and fats are sources of energy, when the glucose levels begin to decrease during prolonged exercise, more fat is used as energy substrate. Equally important is the fact that fat-burning enzymes increase with aerobic training. The role of these enzymes is significant, because fat can only be lost by burning it in muscle. As the concentration of the enzymes increases, so does the ability to burn fat.

Designing Your Own Weight Loss Program

In addition to exercise and adequate food management, many experts still recommend that individuals take a look at their daily caloric intake and compare it against the estimated daily requirement. Your current daily caloric intake can be determined by keeping a record of your daily food intake as has been explained earlier in this chapter (see Figure 4.2). You may also obtain this figure using the computerized nutrient analysis. While this intake may not be as crucial if proper food management and exercise are incorporated into your daily lifestyle, it is still beneficial in certain circumstances. All too often the nutritional analysis reveals that "faithful" dieters are not consuming enough calories and actually need to increase the daily caloric intake (combined with an exercise program) in order to get the metabolism to kick back up to a normal level.

There are other cases where knowledge of the daily caloric requirement is needed for successful weight control. The reasons for prescribing a certain caloric figure to either maintain or lose weight are: (a) it takes time to develop new behaviors and some individuals have difficulty in changing and adjusting to the new eating habits; (b) many individuals are in such poor physical condition that it takes them a long time to increase their aerobic activity level to the point where they will start burning large amounts of calories to aid in faster weight loss; (c) some dieters find it difficult to succeed unless they can count calories; and (d) some individuals will simply not alter their food selection. All of these people can benefit from a caloric intake guideline, and in many instances a sensible caloric decrease is helpful in the early stages of the weight reduction program. For the latter group, that is, those who will not alter their food selection, a significant increase in physical activity, a negative caloric balance, or a combination of both are the only solutions for successful weight loss.

To write your own weight control program, you will need to determine the required daily caloric intake, including exercise, to maintain your current weight. This estimated daily caloric requirement can be determined by using Figure 4.3 and Tables 4.1 and 4.2. Keep in mind that this is only an estimated value, and individual adjustments related to many of the factors discussed in this chapter may be required to establish a more precise value. Nevertheless, the estimated value will provide an initial guideline for weight control and/or reduction.

do this! @

A. Current body weight   10/18
                                                   12/9/92 ___ 95

B. Caloric requirement per pound of body weight
   (use Table 4.1)   __ 13.5 __

C. Typical daily caloric requirement without exercise
   to maintain body weight (A × B)   __ 1283 __

D. Selected physical activity (e.g., jogging)*   ~~~~ aerobics

E. Number of exercise sessions per week   __ 3 __

F. Duration of exercise session (in minutes)   __ per 60 min __

G. Total weekly exercise time in minutes (E × F)   __ 180 __

H. Average daily exercise time in minutes (G ÷ 7)   __ 25.714 __

I. Caloric expenditure per pound per minute
   (cal/lb/min) of physical activity (use Table 4.2)   __ .102 __

J. Total calories burned per minute of physical activity
   (A × I)   __ 9.69 __

K. Average daily calories burned as a result of the
   exercise program (H × J)   __ 249.1686 __

L. Total daily caloric requirement with exercise to
   maintain body weight (C + K)   __ 1532 __

M. Number of calories to subtract from daily requirement to achieve a negative caloric balance**   __ 500 __

N. Target caloric intake to lose weight (L − M)   __ 1032 __

---

* If more than one physical activity is selected, you will need to estimate the average daily calories burned as a result of each additional activity (steps D through K) and add all of these figures to L above.

** Subtract 500 calories if the total daily requirement with exercise (L) is below 3,000 calories. As many as 1,000 calories may be subtracted for daily requirements above 3,000 calories.

FIGURE 4.3. Computation form for daily caloric requirement.

TABLE 4.1. Average caloric requirement per pound of body weight based on lifestyle patterns and gender.

Activity Rating	Calories per pound	
	Men	Women*
Sedentary — Limited physical activity	13.0	12.0
Moderate physical activity	15.0	13.5
Hard Labor — Strenuous physical effort	17.0	15.0

*Pregnant or lactating women: Add three calories to these values.

TABLE 4.2. Caloric expenditure of selected physical activities (calories per pound of body weight per minute of activity).

Activity*	Cal/lb/min	Activity	Cal/lb/min
Aerobic Dance		Running	
Moderate	0.075	11.0 min/mile	0.070
Vigorous	0.095	8.5 min/mile	0.090
Archery	0.030	7.0 min/mile	0.102
Badminton		6.0 min/mile	0.114
Recreation	0.038	Deep water[a]	0.100
Competition	0.065	Skating (moderate)	0.038
Baseball	0.031	Skiing	
Basketball		Downhill	0.060
Moderate	0.046	Level (5 mph)	0.078
Competition	0.063	Soccer	0.059
Cycling (level)		Strength Training	0.050
5.5 mph	0.033	Swimming (crawl)	
10.0 mph	0.050	20 yds/min	0.031
13.0 mph	0.071	25 yds/min	0.040
Bowling	0.030	45 yds/min	0.057
Calisthenics	0.033	50 yds/min	0.070
Dance		Table Tennis	0.030
Moderate	0.030	Tennis	
Vigorous	0.055	Moderate	0.045
Golf	0.030	Competition	0.064
Gymnastics		Volleyball	0.030
Light	0.030	Walking	
Heavy	0.056	4.5 mph	0.045
Handball	0.064	Shallow pool	0.090
Hiking	0.040	Water Aerobics	
Judo/Karate	0.086	Moderate	0.080
Racquetball	0.065	Vigorous	0.100
Rope Jumping	0.060	Wrestling	0.085
Rowing (vigorous)	0.090		

* Values are only for actual time engaged in the activity.   [a]Treading water

Adapted from:
Allsen, P. E., J. M. Harrison, and B. Vance. *Fitness for Life: An Individualized Approach*. Dubuque, IA: Wm. C. Brown, 1989.
Bucher, C. A., and W. E. Prentice, *Fitness for College and Life*. St. Louis: Times Mirror/Mosby College Publishing, 1989.
Consolazio, C. F., R. E. Johnson, and L. J. Pecora. *Physiological measurements of Metabolic Functions in Man*. New York: McGraw-Hill, 1963.
Hockey, R. V. *Physical Fitness: The Pathway to Healthful Living*. St. Louis: Times Mirror/Mosby College Publishing, 1989.

The average daily caloric requirement without exercise is based on typical lifestyle patterns, total body weight, and gender. Individuals who hold jobs that require heavy manual labor burn more calories during the day as opposed to those who hold sedentary jobs, such as working behind a desk. To determine the activity level, refer to Table 4.1 and rate yourself accordingly. Since the number given in this table is per pound of body weight, you will need to multiply your current weight by that number. For example, the typical caloric requirement to maintain body weight for a moderately active male who weighs 160 pounds would be 2,400 calories (160 lbs × 15 cal/lb).

The second step is to determine the average number of calories that are burned on a daily basis as a result of exercise. To obtain this number, you will need to determine the total number of minutes in which you engage in physical activity on a weekly basis, and then compute the daily average exercise time. For instance, a person cycling at thirteen miles per hour, five times per week, for thirty minutes each time, exercises a total of 150 minutes per week (5 × 30). The average daily exercise time would be twenty-one minutes (150 ÷ 7 and round off to the lowest unit). Next, using Table 4.2, determine the energy requirement for the activity (or activities) that has been chosen for the exercise program. In the case of cycling (thirteen miles per hour), the requirement is .071 calories per pound of body weight per minute of activity (cal/lb/min). With a body weight of 160 pounds, this man would burn 11.4 calories each minute (body weight × .071 or 160 × .071). In twenty-one minutes, he would burn approximately 240 calories (21 × 11.4).

The third step is to determine the estimated total caloric requirement, with exercise, needed to maintain body weight. This value is obtained by adding the typical daily requirement (without exercise) and the average calories burned through exercise. In our example, it would be 2,640 calories (2,400 + 240).

If a negative caloric balance is recommended to lose weight, this person would have to consume less than 2,640 daily calories to achieve the objective. Because of the many different factors that play a role in weight control, the previous value is only an estimated daily requirement. Furthermore, to lose weight, it would be difficult to say that exactly one pound of fat would be lost in one week if daily intake was reduced by 500 calories (500 × 7 = 3,500 calories, or the equivalent of one pound of fat). Nevertheless, the estimated daily caloric figure will provide a target guideline for weight control. Periodic readjustments are necessary because there are significant differences among individuals, and the estimated daily requirement will change as you lose weight and modify your exercise habits.

The recommended number of calories to be subtracted from the daily intake to obtain a negative caloric balance depends on the typical daily requirement. At this point, the best recommendation is to moderately decrease the daily intake, never below 1,200 calories for women and 1,500 for men. A good rule to follow is to restrict the intake by no more than 500 calories if the daily requirement is below 3,000 calories. For caloric requirements in excess of 3,000, as many as 1,000 calories per day may be subtracted from the total intake. Remember also that the daily distribution should be approximately 60 percent carbohydrates (mostly complex carbohydrates), less than 30 percent fat, and about 15 percent protein.

The time of day when food is consumed may also play a role in weight reduction. A study conducted at the Aerobics Research Center in Dallas, Texas, indicated that when on a diet, weight is lost most effectively if the majority of the calories are consumed before 1:00 p.m. and not during the evening meal. The recommendation made at this center is that when a person is attempting to lose weight, a minimum of 25 percent of the total daily calories should be consumed for breakfast, 50 percent for lunch, and 25 percent or less at dinner. Other experts have indicated that if most of your daily calories are consumed during one meal, the body may perceive that something is wrong and will slow down your metabolism so that it can store a greater amount of calories in the form of fat. Also, eating most of the calories in one meal causes you to go hungry the rest of the day, making it more difficult to adhere to the diet.

TIPS TO HELP CHANGE BEHAVIOR AND ADHERE TO A LIFETIME WEIGHT MANAGEMENT PROGRAM

Achieving and maintaining ideal body composition is by no means an impossible task, but it does require desire and commitment. If adequate weight management is to become a priority in life, people must realize that some retraining of behavior is crucial for success. Modifying old habits and developing new positive behaviors take time. The following list of management techniques has been successfully used by individuals to change detrimental behavior and adhere to a positive lifetime weight control program. People are not expected to use all of the strategies listed, but they should check the ones that would apply and help them in developing a retraining program.

1. **Commitment to change.** The first ingredient to modify behavior is the desire to do so. The reasons for change must be more important than those for carrying on with present lifestyle patterns. People must accept the fact that there is a problem and decide by themselves whether they really want to change. If a sincere commitment is there, the chances for success are already enhanced.

2. **Set realistic goals.** Most people with a weight problem would like to lose weight in a relatively short period of time but fail to realize that the weight problem developed over a span of several years. In setting a realistic long-term goal, short-term objectives should also be planned. The long-term goal may be a decrease in body fat to 20 percent of total body weight. The short-term objective may be a 1 percent decrease in body fat each month. Such objectives allow for regular evaluation and help maintain motivation and renewed commitment to achieve the long-term goal.

3. **Incorporate exercise into the program.** Selecting enjoyable activities, places, times, equipment, and people to work with enhances exercise adherence. Details on developing a complete exercise program are found in Chapter 3.

4. **Develop healthy eating patterns.** Plan on eating three regular meals per day consistent with the body's nutritional requirements. Learn to differentiate between hunger and appetite. Hunger is the actual physical need for food. Appetite is a desire for food, usually triggered by factors such as stress, habit, boredom, depression, food availability, or just the thought of food itself. Eating only when there is a physical need is wise weight management. In this regard, developing and sticking to a regular meal pattern helps control hunger.

5. **Avoid automatic eating.** Many people associate certain daily activities with eating. For example, people eat while cooking, watching television, reading, or visiting with neighbors. Most of the time, the foods consumed in such situations lack nutritional value or are high in sugar and fat.

6. **Stay busy.** People tend to eat more when they sit around and do nothing. Keeping the mind and body occupied with activities not associated with eating helps decrease the desire to eat. Try walking, cycling, playing sports, gardening, sewing, or visiting a library, a museum, a park, etc. Develop other skills and interests or try something new and exciting to break the routine of life.

7. **Plan your meals ahead of time.** Wise shopping is required to accomplish this objective (by the way, when shopping, do so on a full stomach, since such a practice will decrease impulsive buying of unhealthy foods — and then snacking on the way home). Include whole-grain breads and cereals, fruits and vegetables, low-fat milk and dairy products, lean meats, fish, and poultry.

8. **Cook wisely.** Decrease the use of fat and refined foods in food preparation. Trim all visible fat off meats and remove skin off

poultry prior to cooking. Skim the fat off gravies and soups. Bake, broil, and boil instead of frying. Use butter, cream, mayonnaise, and salad dressings sparingly. Avoid shellfish, coconut oil, palm oil, and cocoa butter. Prepare plenty of bulky foods. Add whole-grain breads and cereals, vegetables, and legumes to most meals. Try fruits for dessert. Beware of soda pop, fruit juices, and fruit-flavored drinks (these beverages are usually high in sugar). Drink plenty of water — at least six glasses a day.

9. **Do not serve more food than can or should be eaten.** Measure the food portions and keep serving dishes away from the table. In this manner, less food is consumed, seconds are more difficult to obtain, and appetite is decreased because food is not visible. People should not be forced to eat when they are satisfied (including children after they have already had a healthy, nutritious serving).

10. **Learn to eat slowly and at the table only.** Eating is one of the pleasures of life, and we need to take time to enjoy it. Eating on the run is detrimental because the body is not given sufficient time to "register" nutritive and caloric consumption, and over-eating usually occurs before the fullness signal is perceived. Always eating at the table also forces people to take time out to eat and will decrease snacking between meals, primarily because of the extra time and effort that are required to sit down and eat. When done eating, do not sit around the table. Clean up and put the food away to avoid unnecessary snacking.

11. **Avoid social binges.** Social gatherings are a common place for self-defeating behavior. Do not feel pressured to eat or drink, nor rationalize in these situations. Choose low-calorie foods and entertain yourself with other activities such as dancing and talking.

12. **Beware of raids on the refrigerator and the cookie jar.** When such occur, attempt to take control of the situation. Stop and think what is taking place. For those who have difficulty in avoiding such raids, environmental management is recommended. Do not bring high-calorie, high-sugar, and/or high-fat foods into the house. If they are brought into the house, they ought to be stored in places where they are difficult to get to or are less visible. If they are unseen or not readily available, there will be less temptation. Keeping them in places like the garage and basement may be sufficient to discourage many people from taking the time and

effort to go get them. By no means should treats be completely eliminated, but all things should be done in moderation.

13. **Practice adequate stress management techniques.** Many people snack and increase food consumption when confronted with stressful situations. Eating is not a stress-releasing activity and can in reality aggravate the problem if weight control is an issue.

14. **Monitor changes and reward accomplishments.** Feedback on fat loss, lean tissue gain, and/or weight loss is a reward in itself. Awareness of changes in body composition also helps reinforce new behaviors. Furthermore, being able to exercise uninterruptedly for fifteen, twenty, thirty, sixty minutes, or swimming a certain distance, running a mile, etc., are all accomplishments that deserve recognition. When certain objectives are met, rewards that are not related to eating are encouraged. Buy new clothing, a tennis racket, a bicycle, exercise shoes, or something else that is special.

15. **Think positive**. Avoid negative thoughts on how difficult it might be to change past behaviors. Instead, think of the benefits that will be reaped, such as feeling, looking, and functioning better, plus enjoying better health and improving the quality of life. Attempt to stay away from negative environments and people who will not be supportive. Those who do not have the same desires and/or encourage self-defeating behaviors should be avoided.

IN CONCLUSION

There is no simple and quick way to take off excessive body fat and keep it off for good. Weight management is accomplished through a lifetime commitment to physical activity and adequate food selection. When engaged in a weight (fat) reduction program, people may also have to moderately decrease caloric intake and implement appropriate strategies to modify unhealthy eating behaviors.

During the process of behavior modification, it is almost inevitable to relapse and engage in past negative behaviors. Nevertheless, making mistakes is human and does not necessarily mean failure. Failure comes to those who give up and do not use previous experiences to build upon and, in turn, develop appropriate skills that will prevent self-defeating behaviors in the future. "If there is a will, there is a way," and those who persist will reap the rewards.

NUTRIENT ANALYSIS
based on Appendix B of the textbook
PHYSICAL FITNESS & WELLNESS
by Werner W.K. Hoeger & Sharon A. Hoeger
Morton Publishing Company, 1990.

Jane Doe   Date: 02-22-1990
Age: 22
Body Weight: 144 lbs (65.3 kg)
Activity Rating: Moderate

Food Intake Day One

Food	Amount	Calo-ries	Pro-tein gm	Fat gm	Sat Fat gm	Cho-les-terol mg	Car-bohy-drate gm	Cal-cium mg	Iron mg	Sodium mg	Vit A I.U.	Thi-amin mg	Ribo-fla-vin mg	Nia-cin mg	Vit C mg
Cocoa/hot/with whole milk	1 cup	218	9.1	9	6.1	33	26	298	0.8	123	318	0.10	0.44	0.4	2
Muffin/blueberry	1 muffin	135	3.0	5	1.5	19	20	54	0.9	198	40	0.10	0.11	0.9	1
Apple/raw	1 med	80	0.3	1	0.0	0	20	10	0.4	1	120	0.04	0.03	0.1	6
Chicken/patty/sandwich	1 sandwich	436	24.8	23	6.1	68	34	44	1.9	2,732	47	0.30	0.26	9.2	4
Potato chips	10 chips	114	1.1	8	2.1	0	10	8	0.4	150	0	0.04	0.01	1.0	3
Milk whole	1 c	159	9.0	9	5.1	34	12	288	0.1	120	350	0.07	0.40	0.2	2
Cookies/choc. chip	4 cookies	206	2.0	12	3.4	28	24	14	0.8	140	40	0.04	0.04	0.4	0
Chocolate/M&M's w/peanuts	1 oz.	145	3.2	7	3.2	0	16	35	0.4	17	15	0.02	0.05	0.9	0
Spaghetti/meat balls/sauce	1 c	332	18.6	12	3.0	75	39	124	3.7	1,009	1,590	0.25	0.30	4.0	22
Tomatoes/raw	.5 med	10	0.5	0	0.0	0	2	6	0.3	2	410	0.03	0.02	0.3	11
Lettuce/head	.75 c sm. chunks	8	0.5	0	0.0	0	2	11	0.3	5	188	0.04	0.04	0.2	4
Dressing/blue cheese	1 tbsp.	77	0.7	8	1.9	4	1	12	0.0	8	32	0.00	0.02	0.0	0
Cola	12 oz.	144	0.0	0	0.0	0	37	27	0.0	30	0	0.00	0.00	0.0	0
Bread/french	2 slice(s)	204	6.4	2	0.4	0	38	30	1.6	406	0	0.20	0.16	1.8	0
Butter	2 tsp	72	0.0	8	0.8	24	0	2	0.0	92	320	0.00	0.00	0.0	0
Ice Cream/vanilla	.5 c	135	3.0	7	4.4	27	14	97	0.1	42	295	0.03	0.14	0.1	1
Totals Day One		2,475	82.2	111	38.0	312	295	1,060	11.7	5,075	3,765	1.3	2.0	19.4	55

Computer software available through Morton Publishing Company, Englewood, Colorado.

FIGURE 4.4. Computerized nutritional analysis.

NUTRIENT ANALYSIS: DAILY ANALYSIS, AVERAGE, AND
RECOMMENDED DIETARY ALLOWANCE (RDA) COMPARISON

	Calo-ries	Pro-tein gm	Fat %	Sat Fat %	Cho-les-terol mg	Car-bohy-drate %	Cal-cium mg	Iron mg	Sodium mg	Vit A I.U.	Thi-amin mg	Ribo-fla-vin mg	Nia-cin mg	Vit C mg
Day One	2,475	82.2	40	14	312	47	1,060	11.7	5,075	3,765	1.3	2.0	19.4	55
Day Two	2,061	68.0	37	12	192	50	732	14.9	2,377	2,143	1.4	1.6	12.4	38
Day Three	2,047	78.2	31	11	511	54	899	10.9	2,560	6,274	1.7	3.0	25.7	112
Three Day Average	2,194	76.1	36	12	338	50	897	12.5	3,337	4,060	1.5	2.2	19.2	68
RDA	1,944+	52.3	<30	<10	<300	50>	800	18.0	1,944	4,000	1.1	1.3	14.0	60

+Estimated caloric value based on gender, current body weight, and activity rating (does not include
additional calories burned through a physical exercise program).

OBSERVATIONS

Daily caloric intake should be distributed in such a way that 50 to 60 percent of the total calories come from carbohydrates and
less than 30 percent of the total calories from fat. Protein intake should be about .8 to 1.5 grams per kilogram of body weight or
about 15 to 20 percent of the total calories. Pregnant women need to consume an additional 30 grams of daily protein, while lactating women should have an extra 20 grams of daily protein, or about 25 and 22 percent of total calories, respectively (these additional grams of protein are already included in the RDA values for pregnant and lactating women). Saturated fats should constitute
less than 10 percent of the total daily caloric intake.

Please note that the daily listings of food intake express the amount of carbohydrates, fat, saturated fat, and protein in grams.
However, on the daily analysis and the RDA, only the amount of protein is given in grams. The amount of carbohydrates, fat, and saturated fat are expressed in percent of total calories. The final percentages are based on the total grams and total calories for all
days analyzed, not from the average of the daily percentages.

If your average intake for protein, fat, saturated fat, cholesterol, or sodium is high, refer to the daily listings and decrease the
intake of foods that are high in those nutrients. If your diet is deficient in carbohydrates, calcium, iron, vitamin A, thiamin, riboflavin, niacin, or vitamin C, refer to the statements below and increase your intake of the indicated foods.

Caloric intake may be too high.

Total fat intake is too high.

Saturated fat intake is too high, which increases your risk for coronary heart disease.

Dietary cholesterol intake is too high. An average consumption of dietary cholesterol above 300 mg/day increases the risk for coronary heart disease. Do you know your blood cholesterol level?

Iron intake is low. Iron containing foods include organ meats such as liver, lean meats, poultry, eggs, seafood, dried peas/beans,
nuts, whole and enriched grains, and green leafy vegetables.

Sodium intake is high.

Computer software available through Morton Publishing Company, Englewood, Colroado.

FIGURE 4.4. Computerized nutritional analysis (continued).

A Healthy Lifestyle Approach | 5

Although most individuals in the United States are firm believers in the benefits of a regular fitness program and positive lifestyle habits as a means to promote better health, most do not reap these benefits because they simply do not know how to implement a healthy lifestyle program that will indeed yield the desired results. Unfortunately, many of the present lifestyle patterns of the American people are such a serious threat to our health that they actually increase the deterioration rate of the human body and often lead to premature illness and mortality.

Scientific evidence has clearly shown that improving the quality and most likely the longevity of our lives is a matter of personal choice. Therefore, in addition to the information already presented in the first four chapters of this book, the materials presented in this chapter have been written to complement your fitness program with a comprehensive healthy lifestyle program. The combination of a fitness program with a healthy lifestyle program has been referred to by the experts as the wellness approach to better health and quality of life.

Wellness has been defined as the constant and deliberate effort to stay healthy and achieve the highest potential for well-being. The concept of wellness incorporates many other components other than those associated with physical fitness, such as proper nutrition, disease prevention, spirituality, smoking cessation, stress management, substance abuse control, safety, and health education (see Figure 5.1).

The difference between physical fitness and wellness is best illustrated in the following example. An individual who is running three miles per day, lifting weights regularly, participating in stretching exercises, and maintaining ideal body weight, can easily be classified in the good or

FIGURE 5.1. Wellness components.

excellent category for each one of the fitness components. However, if this person suffers from high blood pressure, smokes, consumes alcohol, and/or eats a diet high in fatty foods, the individual is probably developing several risk factors for cardiovascular disease and cancer and may not be aware of it. A risk factor is defined as an asymptomatic state that a person has that may lead to disease.

Consequently, the biggest challenge that we are faced with at the end of this century is to teach individuals how to take control of their personal health habits to insure a better, healthier, happier, and more productive life. To help you determine how well your lifestyle habits are contributing to your health, a simple "healthstyle self-test" was developed by the National Health Information Clearinghouse. This self-test is contained in Appendix C and you are encouraged to take the time to fill out this questionnaire.

Researchers have also indicated that practicing seven simple lifestyle habits can significantly increase longevity. These are:

1. Sleeping seven to eight hours each night.

2. Eating breakfast every day.

3. Not eating between meals.

4. Eating less sweets and fat.

5. Maintaining ideal body weight.

6. Exercising regularly.

7. Avoiding chemical use problems (includes drinking only moderate amounts of alcohol or none at all, not smoking cigarettes, and refraining from all other hard drug use).

MAJOR HEALTH PROBLEMS IN THE UNITED STATES

Based on current statistical estimates, the leading causes of death in the country today are basically lifestyle related. About 70 percent of all deaths are caused by cardiovascular disease and cancer. Approximately 80 percent of these could be prevented through a positive lifestyle program. Accidents are the third cause of death. While not all accidents are preventable, many are. A significant amount of fatal accidents are related to alcohol and lack of use of seat belts. The fourth cause of death, chronic obstructive pulmonary disease, is largely related to tobacco use.

CARDIOVASCULAR DISEASE

The most prevalent degenerative diseases in the United States are those of the cardiovascular system. Close to one-half of all deaths in the country result from cardiovascular disease. The disease refers to any pathological condition that affects the heart and the circulatory system (blood vessels). Some examples of cardiovascular diseases are coronary heart disease, peripheral vascular disease, congenital heart disease, rheumatic heart disease, atherosclerosis, strokes, high blood pressure, and congestive heart failure. Table 5.1 provides the estimated prevalence and

TABLE 5.1. Estimated Prevalence and Yearly Number of Deaths from Cardio-vascular Disease

	Prevalence	Deaths
Major forms of cardiovascular diseases*	65,000,000	964,000
Coronary heart disease	5,000,000	**
Heart Attack	1,500,000	550,000
Stroke	2,000,000	150,000
High blood pressure	60,000,000	31,000
Rheumatic heart disease	2,100,000	7,000

   * Includes people with one or more forms of cardiovascular disease.
** Number of deaths included under heart attack.

Sources: American Heart Association and National Center for Health Statistics (U.S. Public Health Service, Department of Health and Human Services).

annual number of deaths caused by the major types of cardiovascular disease.

According to the American Heart Association, heart and blood vessel disease costs were in excess of $83.7 billion in 1985. Heart attacks alone cost American industry 132 million workdays annually, including $12.4 billion in lost productivity because of physical and emotional disability.

It must also be noted that in the case of coronary heart disease, about 50 percent of the time the first symptom of this disease is a heart attack itself. Forty percent of the people who suffer a first heart attack die within the first twenty-four hours. Presently, in one out of every five cardio-vascular deaths, sudden death is the initial symptom. Close to 200,000 of those that die are people in their most productive years between the ages of thirty and sixty-five.

Even though cardiovascular disease is still the leading cause of death in the country, the mortality rates for this disease have been decreasing in the last three decades. In the last few years, approximately 200,000 people were saved each year that were expected to die as a direct result of heart and blood vessel disease. This reduction is attributed primarily to prevention programs dealing with risk factor management and to better health care.

The major form of cardiovascular disease is coronary heart disease (CHD), a condition in which the arteries that supply the heart muscle with oxygen and nutrients are narrowed by fatty deposits such as cholesterol and triglycerides. The narrowing of the coronary arteries diminishes the blood supply to the heart muscle, which can eventually lead to a heart

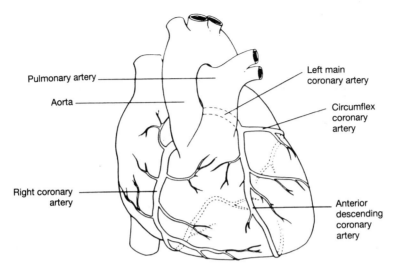

FIGURE 5.2. The heart and its blood vessels (coronary arteries).

attack. CHD is the single leading cause of death in the United States, accounting for approximately one-third of all deaths, and more than half of all cardiovascular deaths.

The leading risk factors that contribute to the development of CHD have been identified and are listed in Table 5.2. An important concept in CHD risk management is that with the exception of age, family history of heart disease, and certain electrocardiogram abnormalities, all of the other risk factors are preventable and reversible and can be controlled by the

---

TABLE 5.2. Leading Risk Factors for Coronary Heart Disease

Elevated Blood Lipids (Cholesterol and Triglycerides)*
Smoking*
High Blood Pressure*
Cardiovascular Endurance
Body Composition
Diabetes
Abnormal Electrocardiogram (ECG)
Tension and Stress
Personal History
Family History
Age

---

*Most significant risk factors

---

individuals themselves through appropriate lifestyle modifications. To aid in the implementation of a lifetime risk reduction program, the following guidelines should be implemented:

Cardiovascular Endurance

Improving cardiovascular endurance through aerobic exercise has perhaps the greatest impact in overall heart disease risk reduction. In this regard, you need to be sure to engage in a lifetime aerobic exercise program, training a minimum of three times per week, in the appropriate target zone, for about 20 to 30 minutes per workout. In the words of Dr. Kenneth H. Cooper, pioneer of the aerobic movement in the United States, the evidence of the benefits of aerobic exercise in the reduction of heart disease is "far too impressive to be ignored." The guidelines for the implementation of an aerobic exercise program are thoroughly discussed in Chapter 3.

Blood Pressure

Blood pressure should be checked regularly, regardless of whether elevation is present or not. Ideal blood pressure should be 120/80 or below. The American Heart Association considers all blood pressures over 140/90 as hypertension. Regular aerobic exercise, weight control, a low-salt low-fat diet, smoking cessation, and stress management are the key principles for blood pressure control.

Body Composition

As discussed in Chapters 2 and 3, body composition refers to the ratio of lean body weight to fat weight. If too much fat is accumulated, the person is considered to be obese. Obesity has long been recognized as a primary risk factor for coronary heart disease. Maintenance of recommended body weight (fat percent) is essential in any cardiovascular risk reduction program.

Blood Lipids

The term "blood lipids" (fats) is mainly used in reference to cholesterol and triglycerides. If you have never had a blood lipid test, it is highly recommended that you have one in the near future. Your blood test should include total cholesterol, HDL-cholesterol (high density lipoprotein cholesterol), and triglycerides. A significant elevation in blood lipids has been clearly linked to heart and blood vessel disease.

Only a few years ago the general recommendation was to keep total blood cholesterol levels below 200 mg/dl (milligrams per deciliter). For individuals thirty and younger it is now recommended that the total cholesterol count should not exceed 180 mg/dl. Even though these guidelines should still be followed, the crucial factor seems to be the way in which cholesterol is "packaged" or carried in the bloodstream rather than the total amount present.

Cholesterol is primarily transported or packaged in the form of high-density lipoprotein cholesterol (HDL-cholesterol) and low-density lipoprotein cholesterol (LDL-cholesterol). The high-density molecules have a high affinity for cholesterol and tend to attract cholesterol, which is then carried to the liver to be metabolized and excreted. In other words, they act as "scavengers" removing cholesterol from the body, thus preventing plaque formation in the arteries. On the other hand, LDL-cholesterol tends to release cholesterol, which may then penetrate the lining of the arteries, enhancing the process of atherosclerosis.

From the previous discussion, it can easily be seen that the more HDL-cholesterol present, the better. HDL-cholesterol is the so called "good cholesterol" and offers a certain degree of protection against heart disease. Many authorities now believe that the ratio of total cholesterol to HDL-cholesterol is a better indicator of potential risk for cardiovascular disease than the total value by itself. It is generally accepted that a 4.5 or lower ratio (total cholesterol/HDL-cholesterol) is excellent for men, and 4.0 or lower is best for women. For instance, 50 mg/dl of HDL-cholesterol as compared to 200 mg/dl of total cholesterol yields a ratio of 4.0 (200 ÷ 50 = 4.0).

New evidence also indicates that low levels of HDL-cholesterol could be the best predictor of coronary heart disease, and seems to be more significant than the total value itself. Researchers at the 1988 annual American Heart Association meeting indicated that people with low total cholesterol (less than 200 mg/dl) and also low HDL-cholesterol (under 40 mg/dl) may have three times the heart disease risk of those with high cholesterol but with good HDL-cholesterol levels. HDL-cholesterol levels in the high 40s (or higher), therefore, seem to offer the best protection.

As a general rule of thumb, the following dietary guidelines are recommended to lower LDL-cholesterol levels: (a) egg consumption should be limited to less than three eggs per week; (b) red meats should be eaten less than three times per week, and organ meats (e.g., liver and kidneys), sausage, bacon, hot dogs, and canned meats should be avoided; (c) low-fat milk (1 percent or less preferably) and low-fat dairy products are recommended; (d) shellfish, coconut oil, palm oil, and cocoa butter should be avoided or used sparingly; and (e) ideal body composition should be achieved. Aerobic exercise is also crucial, because it helps increase HDL-cholesterol.

Triglycerides are carried in the bloodstream primarily by very low-density lipoproteins (VLDL) and chylomicrons. These fatty acids are found in poultry skin, lunch meats, and shellfish. However, they are mainly manu-factured in the liver from refined sugars, starches, and alcohol. High intake of alcohol and sugars (honey included) will significantly increase tri-glyceride levels. Thus, they can be lowered by decreasing the consumption of the above-mentioned foods along with weight reduction (if overweight) and aerobic exercise. An optimal blood triglyceride level is less than 100 mg/dl.

Diabetes

Diabetes is a condition in which the blood glucose is unable to enter the cells because of insufficient insulin production by the pancreas. Sev-eral studies have shown that the incidence of cardiovascular disease among diabetic patients is quite high. Cardiovascular disease is also the leading cause of death among these patients.

Although there is a genetic predisposition to diabetes, adult-onset diabetes is closely related to obesity. In most cases, this type of condition can be corrected by following a special diet, a weight loss program, and exercise. If you have elevated blood glucose levels, you should consult your physician and let him/her decide on the best approach to treat this condition.

Electrocardiograms (ECG)

The ECG provides a record of the electrical impulses that stimulate the heart to contract. ECGs are taken at rest and during stress of exercise. A stress ECG is also known as a maximal exercise tolerance test. Similar to a high-speed road test on a car, a stress ECG reveals the tolerance of the heart to high-intensity exercise. Based on the findings, ECGs may be inter-preted as normal, equivocal, or abnormal.

A stress ECG is frequently used to diagnose coronary heart disease. It is also used to determine cardiovascular fitness levels, to screen persons for preventive and cardiac rehabilitation programs, to detect abnormal blood pressure response during exercise, and to establish actual or func-tional maximal heart rate for exercise prescription purposes.

While not every adult who wishes to start an exercise program needs a stress ECG, the following guidelines can be used to determine when this type of test should be administered:

- Adults forty-five years or older.

- A total cholesterol level above 200 mg/dl, or a total cholesterol/HDL-cholesterol ratio above 4.0 for women and 4.5 for men.

- Hypertensive and diabetic patients.

- Cigarette smokers.

- Individuals with a family history of coronary heart disease, syncope, or sudden death before age sixty.

- All individuals with symptoms of chest discomfort, dysrhythmias, syncope, or chronotropic incompetence (a heart rate that increases slowly during exercise and never reaches maximum).

Smoking

Cigarette smoking is the single largest preventable cause of illness and premature death in the United States. When considering all related deaths, smoking is responsible for over 250,000 unnecessary deaths each year. There is a definite increase in death rates from heart disease, cancer, stroke, aortic aneurysm, chronic bronchitis, emphysema, and peptic ulcers.

In relation to cardiovascular disease, cigarette smoking not only speeds up the process of atherosclerosis (fatty build-up on the walls of the arteries), but there is also a threefold increase in the risk of sudden death following a myocardial infarction. Smoking increases heart rate, blood pressure, and the irritability of the heart, which can trigger fatal cardiac arrhythmias. Experts have indicated that as far as the extra load on the heart is concerned, giving up one pack of cigarettes per day is the equivalent of losing between fifty and seventy-five pounds of excess body fat! Another harmful effect of cigarette smoking is a decrease in HDL-cholesterol, or the "good type" that helps control blood lipids.

Pipe and/or cigar smoking and chewing tobacco also increase risk for heart disease. Even if no smoke is inhaled, certain amounts of toxic substances can be absorbed through the mouth membranes and end up in the bloodstream. Individuals who use tobacco in any of these three forms also have a much greater risk for cancer of the oral cavity.

Cigarette smoking, poor total cholesterol/HDL-cholesterol ratio, and high blood pressure are the three most significant risk factors for coronary disease. Nevertheless, the risk for both cardiovascular disease and cancer starts to decrease the moment you quit smoking. The risk approaches that of a lifetime nonsmoker ten and fifteen years, respectively, following cessation.

Quitting cigarette smoking is no easy task. Only about 20 percent of smokers who try to quit for the first time each year succeed. The addictive properties of nicotine and smoke make it very difficult to quit. Smokers experience physical and psychological withdrawal symptoms when they stop smoking. While giving up smoking can be extremely difficult, cessation is by no means an impossible task.

The most important factor in quitting cigarette smoking is the person's sincere desire to do so. More than 95 percent of the successful ex-smokers have been able to quit on their own, either by quitting cold turkey or by using self-help kits available from organizations such as the American Cancer Society, the American Heart Association, and the American Lung Association. Only three percent of ex-smokers have quit as a result of formal cessation programs. A six-step plan to help people stop smoking is contained in Figure 5.3.

Tension and Stress

Tension and stress have become a normal part of every person's life. Everyone has to deal with daily goals, deadlines, responsibilities, pressures, etc. Almost everything in life (whether positive or negative) is a source of stress. However, it is not the stressor itself that creates the health hazard, but rather the individual's response to it that may pose a health problem. Individuals who are under a lot of stress and cannot relax will experience a constant low-level strain on the cardiovascular system that could manifest itself in the form of heart disease.

Learning to live and get ahead today is practically impossible without practicing adequate stress management techniques. Perhaps the two easiest stress management techniques available are physical exercise and breathing techniques.

Physical exercise is one of the simplest tools used to control stress. The value of exercise in reducing stress is related to several factors, the principal one being a decrease in muscular tension. For example, a person may be distressed because he/she had a miserable day at work, and the job required eight hours of work in a smoke-filled room with an intolerable boss. To make matters worse, it is late and on the way home the car in front is going much slower than the speed limit. The body's "fight or flight" mechanism is activated, heart rate and blood pressure shoot up, breathing quickens and deepens, muscles tense up, and all systems say "go." But no action can be initiated, nor stress dissipated, because you just cannot hit your boss or the car in front of you. However, a person could surely take action by "hitting" the tennis ball, the weights, the swimming pool, or the jogging trail. By engaging in physical activity, a person is able to reduce the muscular tension and eliminate the physiological changes that triggered the "fight or flight" mechanism.

Breathing exercises can also be used as an antidote to stress. Such exercises have been used for centuries in the Orient and India as a means to develop better mental, physical, and emotional stamina. In breathing

Six-Step Smoking Cessation Approach

The following six-step plan has been developed as a guide to help you quit smoking. The total program should be completed in four weeks or less. Steps one through four should take no longer than two weeks. A maximum of two additional weeks are allowed for the rest of the program.

Step One. The first step in breaking the habit is to decide positively that you want to quit. Now prepare a list of the reasons why you smoke and why you want to quit.

Step Two. Initiate a personal diet and exercise program. Exercise and decreased body weight cause a greater awareness of healthy living and increase motivation for giving up cigarettes.

Step Three. Decide on the approach that you will use to stop smoking. You may quit cold turkey or gradually decrease the number of cigarettes smoked daily. Many people have found that quitting cold turkey is the easiest way to do it. While it may not work the first time, after several attempts, all of a sudden smokers are able to overcome the habit without too much difficulty. Tapering off cigarettes can be done in several ways. You may start by eliminating cigarettes that you do not necessarily need, you can switch to a brand lower in nicotine and/or tar every couple of days, you can smoke less off each cigarette, or you can simply decrease the total number of cigarettes smoked each day.

Step Four. Set the target date for quitting. In setting the target date, choosing a special date may add a little extra incentive. An upcoming birthday, anniversary, vacation, graduation, family reunion, etc., are all examples of good dates to free yourself from smoking.

Step Five. Stock up on low-calorie foods — carrots, broccoli, cauliflower, celery, popcorn (butter and salt free), fruits, sunflower seeds (in the shell), sugarless gum, and plenty of water. Keep such food handy on the day you stop and the first few days following cessation. Replace such food for cigarettes when you want one.

Step Six. This is the day that you will quit smoking. On this day and the first few days thereafter, do not keep cigarettes handy. Stay away from friends and events that trigger your desire to smoke. You should drink large amounts of water, fruit juices, and eat low calorie foods. An important factor in breaking the habit is to replace the old behavior with new behavior. You will need to replace smoking time with new positive substitutes that will make smoking difficult or impossible. When you desire a cigarette, take a few deep breaths and then occupy yourself by doing a number of things such as talking to someone else, washing your hands, brushing your teeth, eating a healthy snack, chewing on a straw, doing dishes, playing sports, going for a walk or bike ride, going swimming, and so on.

If you have been successful and stopped smoking, remember that there are a lot of events that can still trigger your urge to smoke. When confronted with such events, people rationalize and think, "One will not hurt." It will not work! Before you know, you will be back to the regular nasty habit. Therefore, be prepared to take action in those situations. Find adequate substitutes for smoking. Remind yourself of how difficult it has been and how long it has taken you to get to this point. Keep in mind that it will only get easier rather than worse as time goes on.

FIGURE 5.3.

exercises, the person concentrates on "breathing away" the tension and inhaling fresh oxygen to the entire body. Breathing exercises can be learned in only a few minutes and require considerably less time than other forms of stress management. An example of such exercises are given in Figure 5.4.

Personal and Family History

Individuals who have a family history or have already suffered from cardiovascular problems are at higher risk than those who have never had a problem. People with such a history should be strongly encouraged to maintain the other risk factors as low as possible. Since most risk factors are reversible, this practice significantly decreases the risk for future problems.

Breathing Exercises for Stress Management

A quiet, pleasant, and well-ventilated room should be used to perform breathing exercises. Any of the three exercises listed below may be performed whenever tension is felt due to stress.

Deep breathing: Lie with your back flat against the floor, place a pillow under your knees, feet slightly separated, with toes pointing outward (the exercise may also be conducted sitting up in a chair or standing straight up). Place one hand on your abdomen and the other one on your chest. Slowly breathe in and out so that the hand on your abdomen rises when you inhale and falls as you exhale. The hand on the chest should not move much at all. Repeat the exercise about ten times. Next, scan your body for tension, and compare your present tension with that felt at the beginning of the exercise. Repeat the entire process once or twice more.

Sighing: Using the abdominal breathing technique, breathe in through your nose to a specific count (i.e., 4, 5, 6, etc.). Now exhale through pursed lips to double the intake count (i.e., 8, 10, 12, etc.). Repeat the exercise eight to ten times whenever you feel tense.

Complete natural breathing: Sit in an upright position or stand straight up. Breathe through your nose and gradually fill up your lungs from the bottom up. Hold your breath for several seconds. Now exhale slowly by allowing complete relaxation of the chest and abdomen. Repeat the exercise eight to ten times.

FIGURE 5.4.

Age

Age is a risk factor because of the greater incidence of heart disease among older people. This tendency may be partly induced by an increased risk among the other factors due to changes in lifestyle as we get older (less physical activity, poor nutrition, obesity, etc.).

Young people, however, should not feel that heart disease will not affect them. The disease process begins early in life. Autopsies conducted on young people who died in their twenties have revealed early stages of atherosclerosis. Other studies have found elevated blood cholesterol levels in children as young as ten years old.

While the aging process cannot be stopped, it can certainly be slowed down. It has often been said that certain individuals in their sixties or older possess the bodies of twenty-year-olds. The opposite also holds true: Twenty-year-olds often are in such poor condition and health that they almost seem to have the bodies of sixty-year-olds. Adequate risk factor management and positive lifestyle habits are the best ways to slow down the natural aging process.

CANCER

Cancer is defined as an uncontrolled growth and spread of abnormal cells in the body. Some cells grow into a mass of tissue called a tumor, which can be either benign or malignant. A malignant tumor would be considered a "cancer". If the spread of cells is not controlled, death ensues. Over 22 percent of all deaths in the United States are due to cancer. An estimated one million new cases are reported and about a half a million people die each year from cancer.

As with cardiovascular disease, cancer is largely a preventable disease. The biggest factor in fighting cancer today is health education. As much as 80 percent of all human cancers are related to lifestyle or environmental factors (includes diet, tobacco use, excessive use of alcohol, overexposure to sunlight, and exposure to occupational hazards). Most of these cancers could be prevented through positive lifestyle habits.

Equally important is the fact that cancer is now viewed as the most curable of all chronic diseases. Over half of all cancers are curable. Over five million Americans were alive in 1989 who had a history of cancer. Close to three million of them were considered cured.

The most effective way to protect against cancer is by changing negative lifestyle habits and behaviors that have been practiced for years. The American Cancer Society has issued the following recommendations in regard to cancer prevention (also see Figure 5.5):

ARE YOU TAKING CONTROL?

Today, scientists think most cancers may be related to lifestyle and environment — what you eat, drink, if you smoke and where you work and play. So the good news is you can help reduce your own cancer risk by taking control of things in your daily life.

10 Steps To A Healthier Life and Reduced Cancer Risk

1. **Are you eating more cabbage-family vegetables?**
   They include broccoli, cauliflower, brussels sprouts, all cabbages and kale.   ☐ ☐

2. **Are high-fiber foods included in your diet?**
   Fiber occurs in whole grains, fruits and vegetables including peaches, strawberries, potatoes, spinach, tomatoes, wheat and bran cereals, rice, popcorn and whole-wheat bread.   ☐ ☐

3. **Do you choose foods with Vitamin A?**
   Fresh foods with beta-carotene like carrots, peaches, apricots, squash and broccoli are the best source, not vitamin pills.   ☐ ☐

4. **Is Vitamin C included in your diet?**
   You'll find it naturally in lots of fresh fruits and vegetables like grapefruit, cantaloupe, oranges, strawberries, red and green peppers, broccoli and tomatoes.   ☐ ☐

5. **Do you exercise and monitor calorie intake to avoid weight gain?**
   Walking is ideal exercise for many people.   ☐ ☐

6. **Are you cutting overall fat intake?**
   This is done by eating lean meat, fish, skinned poultry and low-fat dairy products.   ☐ ☐

7. **Do you limit salt-cured, smoked, nitrite-cured foods?**
   Choose bacon, ham, hot dogs or salt-cured fish only occasionally if you like them a lot.   ☐ ☐

8. **If you smoke, have you tried quitting?**   ☐ ☐

9. **If you drink alcohol, are you moderate in your intake?**   ☐ ☐

10. **Do you respect the sun's rays?**
    Protect yourself with sunscreen — at least #15, wear long sleeves and a hat, especially during midday hours — 11 a.m. to 3 p.m.   ☐ ☐

If you answer yes to most of these questions, **Congratulations.** You are taking control of simple lifestyle factors that will help you feel better and reduce your cancer risk.

*Courtesy of the Texas Division of the American Cancer Society.

FIGURE 5.5. Cancer prevention questionnaire.

Dietary Changes

The diet should be low in fat and high in fiber, with ample amounts of vitamins A and C from natural sources. Cruciferous vegetables are encouraged in the diet, alcohol should be used in moderation, and obesity should be avoided.

High fat intake has been linked primarily to breast, colon, and prostate cancers. Low fiber intake seems to increase the risk of colon cancer. Foods high in vitamins A and C may help decrease the incidence of larynx, esophagus, and lung cancers. Additionally, salt-cured, smoked, and nitrite-cured foods should be avoided. These foods have been linked to cancer of the esophagus and stomach. Vitamin C seems to help decrease the formation of nitrosamines (cancer-causing substances that are formed when cured meats are eaten). Cruciferous vegetables (cauliflower, broccoli, Brussels sprouts, and kohlrabi) should be included in the diet, since they seem to decrease the risk for the development of certain cancers.

Alcohol should be used in moderation. Alcoholism increases the risk of certain cancers, especially when combined with tobacco smoking or smokeless tobacco. In combination, they significantly increase the risk of mouth, larynx, throat, esophagus, and liver cancers. According to some research, the synergistic action of heavy use of alcohol and tobacco yields a fifteen-fold increase in cancer of the oral cavity.

Maintenance of ideal body weight is also recommended. Obesity has been associated with colon, rectum, breast, prostate, gallbladder, ovary, and uterine cancers.

Abstinence From Cigarette Smoking

It has been reported that 83 percent of all lung cancer and 30 percent of all cancers are attributed to smoking. Smokeless tobacco also increases the risk of mouth, larynx, throat, and esophagus cancers. Nearly 148,000 cancer deaths annually are attributed to the use of tobacco. The average life expectancy for a chronic smoker is seven years less than for a non-smoker.

Avoid Sun Exposure

Sunlight exposure is a major factor in the development of skin cancer. Almost 100 percent of the 500,000 nonmelanoma skin cancer cases reported annually in the United States are related to sun exposure. Sunscreen lotion should be used at all times when the skin is going to be exposed to sunlight for extended periods of time. Tanning of the skin is the body's natural reaction to cell damage taking place as a result of excessive sun exposure.

Avoid Estrogen Use, Radiation Exposure, and Occupational Hazard Exposure

Estrogen use has been linked to endometrial cancer but can be taken safely under careful physician supervision. Radiation exposure also increases cancer risk. Many times, however, the benefits of X-ray use outweigh the risk involved, and most medical facilities use the lowest dose possible to decrease the risk to a minimum. Occupational hazards, such as asbestos fibers, nickel and uranium dusts, chromium compounds, vinyl chloride, bischlormethyl ether, etc., increase cancer risk. The risk of occupational hazards is significantly magnified by the use of cigarette smoking.

Equally important is the fact that through early detection, many cancers can be controlled or cured. The real problem is the spreading of cancerous cells. Once spreading occurs, it becomes very difficult to wipe the cancer out. It is therefore crucial to practice effective prevention or at least catch cancer when the possibility of cure is greatest. Herein lies the importance of proper periodic screening for prevention and/or early detection.

Warning Signals For Cancer

The following are the seven warning signals for cancer. Every individual should become familiar with these warning signals and bring them to the attention of a physician if any of them are present:

1. Change in bowel or bladder habits.
2. A sore that does not heal.
3. Unusual bleeding or discharge.
4. Thickening or lump in breast or elsewhere.
5. Indigestion or difficulty in swallowing.
6. Obvious change in wart or mole.
7. Nagging cough or hoarseness.

Scientific evidence and testing procedures for prevention and/or early detection of cancer do change. Results of current clinical and epidemiologic studies provide constant new information about cancer prevention and detection. The purpose of cancer prevention programs is to educate and guide individuals toward a lifestyle that will aid them in the prevention and/or early detection of malignancy. Treatment of cancer should always be left to specialized physicians and cancer clinics.

ACCIDENTS

Most people do not perceive accidents as being a health problem, but accidents are the third leading cause of death in the United States, affecting the total well-being of millions of Americans each year. Accident prevention and personal safety are also part of a health enhancement program aimed at achieving a higher quality of life. Proper nutrition, exercise, abstinence from cigarette smoking, and stress management are of little help if the person is involved in a disabling or fatal accident due to distraction, a single reckless decision, or not properly wearing safety seat belts.

Accidents do not just happen. We cause accidents and we are victims of accidents. Although some factors in life are completely beyond our control, such as earthquakes, tornadoes, or airplane crashes, more often than not, personal safety and accident prevention are a matter of common sense. A majority of accidents are the result of poor judgment and confused mental states. Accidents frequently happen when we are upset, not paying attention to the task with which we are involved, or by abusing alcohol and other drugs.

Alcohol abuse is the number one cause of all accidents. Statistics clearly show that alcohol intoxication is the leading cause of most fatal automobile accidents. Other drugs commonly abused in society alter feelings and perceptions, lead to mental confusion, and impair judgment and coordination, thereby greatly enhancing the risk for accidental morbidity and mortality.

CHRONIC OBSTRUCTIVE PULMONARY DISEASE

Chronic obstructive pulmonary disease (COPD) is a term used to describe an air-flow-limiting disease that includes chronic bronchitis, emphysema, and a reactive airway component similar to that of asthma. The incidence of COPD increases proportionally with cigarette smoking (or other forms of tobacco use) and exposure to certain types of industrial pollution. In the case of emphysema, genetic factors may also play a role.

SPIRITUAL WELL-BEING

The scientific association between spirituality and health is more difficult to establish than that of other lifestyle factors such as alcohol, smoking, physical inactivity, seat belt use, etc. Several research studies, nonetheless, have reported a positive relationship between spiritual well-being, emotional well-being, life's satisfaction, and health. One particular study indicated a much higher rate of heart attacks among nonreligious people as compared to a religious sample attending church. Other studies

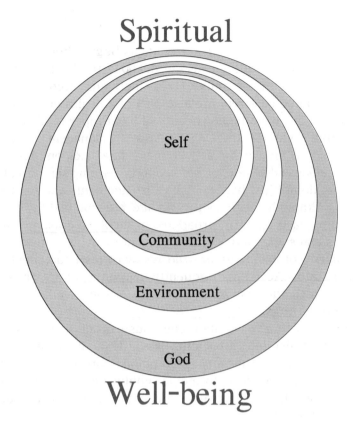

FIGURE 5.6. Spiritual Well-being. An affirmation of life in a relationship with God, self, community, and environment that nurtures and celebrates wholeness.

suggest that religious support may act as a buffer against disease and that the social support encourages preventive health.

Spiritual well-being is defined by the National Interfaith Coalition on Aging as an affirmation of life in a relationship with God, self, community, and environment that nurtures and celebrates wholeness. Because this definition includes Christians and non-Christians alike, it assumes that all people are spiritual in nature.

Wellness requires a balance between physical, mental, spiritual, emotional, and social well-being. The relationship between spirituality and wellness, therefore, is meaningful in man's quest for a better quality of life. Religion has been a major part of cultures since the beginning of time. While not everyone in the United States claims affiliation to a certain religion or denomination, current surveys indicate that 94 percent of the

U.S. population believes in God or a Universal spirit who functions as God. People, furthermore, believe to different extents that (a) a relationship with God is meaningful; (b) God can grant help, guidance, and assistance in daily living; and (c) that there is a purpose to the mortal existence. If we accept any or all of these statements, then attaining the proper degree of spirituality will have a definite effect on a person's happiness and well-being.

SUBSTANCE ABUSE CONTROL (CHEMICAL HEALTH)

Chemical dependency presently includes some of the most serious, self-destructive forms of addiction in our society; including alcohol, hard drugs, and cigarette smoking (the latter has already been discussed in this chapter). Other problems associated with substance abuse include drunken or impaired driving, mixing prescriptions, family problems, and drugs to improve athletic performance.

Alcohol is one of the most significant health-related drug problems in the United States today. Estimates indicate that seven in ten adults, or over 100 million Americans eighteen years and older, are drinkers. Approximately 10 million of them will experience a drinking problem, including alcoholism, in their lifetime. Another 3 million teenagers are thought to have a drinking problem.

Alcohol intake reduces peripheral vision, decreases visual and hearing acuity, decreases reaction time, impairs concentration and motor performance (including increased swaying and impaired judgment of distance and speed of moving objects), decreases fear, increases risk-taking behaviors, increases urination, and induces sleep. A single large dose of alcohol may also decrease sexual function. One of the most unpleasant, dangerous, and life-threatening effects of drinking is the synergistic action of alcohol when combined with other drugs, particularly central nervous system depressants.

Long-term effects of alcohol include cirrhosis of the liver (scarring of the liver which is often fatal); increased risk for oral, esophageal, and liver cancer; cardiomyopathy (a disease that affects the heart muscle); elevated blood pressure; increased risk for strokes; inflammation of the esophagus, stomach, small intestine, and pancreas; stomach ulcers; sexual impotence; malnutrition; brain cell damage leading to loss of memory; psychosis; depression; and hallucinations.

In terms of illegal drugs, estimates indicate that approximately 60 percent of the world's production of such drugs is consumed in the United States. Each year Americans spend over $100 billion on illegal drugs, an amount that surpasses the total amount taken in from all crops by United

States farmers. Based on reports from the U.S. Department of Education, today's drugs are stronger, more addictive, and pose a greater risk than ever before. Drugs lead to physical and psychological dependence. With regular use, they integrate into the body's chemistry, increasing drug tolerance and forcing the user to constantly increase the dosage to obtain similar results. Drug abuse leads not only to serious health problems, but over half of all adolescent suicides are drug-related.

Recognizing that chemical use is a significant part of life in our society is important to us all. Within the context of chemical health, families, teams, and communities can assist each other in preventing problems, as well as assist those experiencing chemical use problems. Treatment of chemical dependency (including alcohol), nevertheless, is seldom accomplished without professional guidance and support. To secure the best available assistance, you need to contact a physician or obtain a referral from your local mental/health clinic. (See Yellow Pages in the phone book.)

SEXUALLY TRANSMITTED DISEASES

Sexually transmitted diseases (STDs) have become an epidemic of national proportions in the United States. There are now over twenty-five known STDs, some of which are still incurable. According to the Centers for Disease Control in Atlanta, in 1986 more than 10 million new people were infected with STDs, including 4.6 million cases of chlamydia, 1.8 million of gonorrhea, 1 million of genital warts, half a million of herpes, 90,000 of syphilis, and attracting most of the attention because of its life-threatening potential were 15,000 new cases of AIDS or Acquired Immune Deficiency Syndrome. The American Social Health Association indicates that 25 percent of all Americans will acquire at least one STD in their lifetime.

AIDS is the most frightening of all STDs because there is no known cure and few victims have survived the disease. Anywhere from 1.5 to 4 million Americans are thought to carry the HIV or AIDS virus. This virus attacks cells, weakening their immune system. Even if an infected person doesn't develop AIDS, he/she can still pass the virus on to others who could easily develop the disease (including pregnant women to their unborn babies). Government estimates indicate that unless an appropriate cure is found, the outlook is bleak. It is projected that by the year 2,000 more than 200,000 people will die from AIDS, making it the third leading cause of death behind cardiovascular disease and cancer.

Many people feel that only certain "high risk groups" of people are infected by the AIDS virus. This is untrue. Who you are has nothing to do with whether you are in danger of being infected with the AIDS virus. What matters is what you do.

High-risk individuals for AIDS are primarily homosexual males with multiple sexual partners and intravenous drug users, but health experts feel that in future years the disease may become just as common among heterosexuals. The virus is transmitted through blood and semen during sexual intercourse or by using hypodermic needles previously used by an infected individual. Anal intercourse, with or without a condom, is risky because the rectum is easily injured during anal intercourse.

AIDS cannot be contracted through everyday contact with people around you in school, in the workplace, at parties, child care centers, or stores. You will not get it by shaking hands with an infected person, from a toilet seat, from dishes or silverware used by an AIDS patient, by using a towel or clothes from a person with AIDS, or from donating blood. Furthermore, you will not get AIDS in a swimming pool, even if someone in the pool is infected with the AIDS virus. Students attending school with someone infected with the AIDS virus are not in danger from casual contact.

Once a person becomes infected with the AIDS virus, there will be an incubation period ranging from a few months to six years during which no symptoms appear. The virus weakens and incapacitates the immune system, leaving the victim vulnerable to all types of infectious diseases and certain types of cancer. The AIDS virus itself doesn't kill, but the ineffectiveness of the immune system in dealing with the various illnesses is what leads to death. Although several drugs are being tested to treat and slow down the disease process, there is no known cure for AIDS.

What about dating? Dating and getting to know other people is a normal part of life. Dating, however, does not mean the same thing as having sex. Sexual intercourse as a part of dating can be risky. One of the risks is AIDS. There is no way for you to tell if someone you are dating or would like to date has been exposed to the AIDS virus. The good news, nonetheless, is that as long as sexual activity and sharing drug needles are avoided, it does not matter who you date.

The best way to prevent sexually transmitted diseases is through a mutually monogamous sexual relationship. In other words, you have sexual relationships with only one person, who has sexual relationships only with you. Risky behaviors that will significantly increase your chances of contracting sexually transmitted diseases, including AIDS, are: (a) multiple and/or anonymous sexual partners including a pickup or prostitute; (b) anal sex with or without a condom; (c) vaginal or oral sex with someone who shoots drugs or engages in anal sex; (d) sex with someone you know has several sex partners; (e) unprotected sex (without a condom) with an infected person; (f) sexual contact (this includes open-mouthed or French kissing, since the AIDS virus may be present in saliva; it should be noted, however, that there is no evidence that AIDS has been transmitted in this way) with anyone who has symptoms of AIDS or who is a member of a high-risk group for AIDS, and (g) sharing toothbrushes, razors, or other implements that could become contaminated with blood with anyone who is, or who might be, infected with the AIDS virus.

IN CONCLUSION

Keep in mind that adequate fitness and total well-being is a process and you need to put forth a constant and deliberate effort to achieve and maintain a higher quality of life. To make your journey easier, remember to enjoy yourself and have fun along the way. If you implement your program based on what you enjoy doing most, adhering to a new lifestyle will not be difficult.

Hopefully, taking part in a fitness and wellness program will help you develop positive "addictions" that will carry on throughout life. If you participate regularly and apply many of the principles explained in this book, you will truly experience a "new quality of life." Once you "reach the top," you will know that there is no looking back. But, if you do not get there, you will never know what it is like. Improving the quality and most likely the longevity of your life is now in your hands. It may require persistence and commitment, but only you can take control of your lifestyle and thereby reap the benefits of wellness.

Relevant Questions Related to Fitness and Wellness . . . and the Answers

6

The purpose of this last chapter is to answer some of the most frequently asked questions regarding different aspects of physical fitness and wellness. The answers to many of the questions will help clarify to an even greater extent different concepts discussed throughout the book, as well as put to rest several myths that misinform fitness and wellness participants.

SAFETY OF EXERCISE PARTICIPATION AND INJURY PREVENTION

- **Can aerobic exercise make a person immune to heart and blood vessel disease?**

Scientific evidence clearly indicates that aerobically fit individuals have a much lower incidence of cardiovascular disease. A regular aerobic exercise program by itself, however, is not an absolute guarantee against diseases of the heart and the blood vessels. Keep in mind that there are several factors that increase a person's risk for cardiovascular disease.

While physical inactivity is one of the most significant risk factors, studies have also documented that multiple interrelations usually exist between these risk factors. Physical inactivity, for instance, often contributes to an increase in (a) body weight (fat), (b) total cholesterol/HDL-cholesterol ratio, (c) triglycerides, (d) tension and stress, (e) blood pressure, and (f) risk for diabetes (see Figure 6.1). As was previously discussed in Chapter 5, most risk factors are preventable and reversible. Overall risk factor management is the best guideline to minimize the risk

Fitness and Wellness

for cardiovascular disease. Research, however, also indicates that the odds of surviving a heart attack are much greater for people who engage in a regular aerobic exercise program.

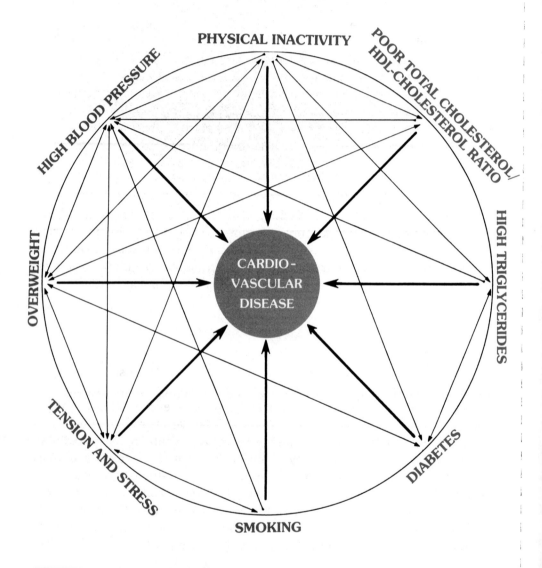

Adapted from Johnson, L.C. Interpreting your test results. Fitness Monitoring, Inc. Fontana, WI, 1981.

FIGURE 6.1. Interrelationships among leading cardiovascular risk factors.

■ **What is the optimal amount of aerobic exercise recommended to significantly decrease the risk for cardiovascular disease?**

The basic principles of cardiovascular exercise prescription were introduced in Chapter 3. The required amount of exercise to maintain cardiovascular endurance is a training session every forty-eight hours for twenty to thirty minutes in the appropriate target zone.

Some researchers, nevertheless, indicate that to obtain a certain degree of protection against cardiovascular disease, approximately 300 calories should be expended on a daily basis through aerobic exercise. Dr. Thomas K. Cureton, in his book *The Physiological Effects of Exercise Programs Upon Adults*, reports that 300 calories per exercise session provide the necessary stimuli to control blood fats (cholesterol and triglycerides), which are a primary risk factor for atherosclerosis, coronary heart disease, and strokes. Dr. Ralph Paffenbarger and co-researchers in their study "Cause-Specific Death Rates per 10,000 Man-Years of Observation Among 16,936 Harvard Alumni, 1962 to 1978, by physical Activity Index" showed that 2,000 calories expended per week as a result of physical activity yielded the lowest risk for cardiovascular disease among this group of almost 17,000 Harvard alumni. Two thousand calories per week represents about 300 calories per daily exercise session.

■ **At what age should I start concerning myself with heart disease?**

The disease process, not only for cardiovascular disease, but also cancer, starts early in life as a result of poor lifestyle habits. Studies have shown beginning stages of atherosclerosis and elevated blood lipids in children as young as ten years old. Many positive lifestyle habits can be established early in life within the walls of your own home. If children are taught at a young age that they should avoid excessive calories, sweets, salt, tobacco, alcohol, and participate in physical activity, their chances of leading a healthier life are much greater than the present generation. And remember some of the best advice given to mankind when it comes to teaching: "come and follow me." If you practice positive health habits in your own life, your children will be more likely to follow.

■ **Can I exercise after donating blood?**

The average amount taken when a person donates blood is about 500 ml (a half-liter) out of a total volume of five liters. This volume is immediately replenished by reserve blood components stored in the body. Unless you are given special instructions not to exercise, there is no reason why you cannot continue with your regular program.

■ Will exercise offset the detrimental effects of cigarette smoking?

Physical exercise often motivates toward smoking cessation but does not offset any ill effects of smoking. If anything, smoking greatly decreases the ability of the blood to transport oxygen to working muscles. Oxygen is carried in the circulatory system by hemoglobin, the iron-containing pigment of the red blood cells. Carbon monoxide, a by-product of cigarette smoke, has 210 to 250 times greater affinity for hemoglobin than oxygen. Consequently, carbon monoxide combines much faster with hemoglobin, decreasing the oxygen-carrying capacity of the blood.

Chronic smoking also increases airway resistance, requiring the respiratory muscles to work much harder and consume more oxygen just to ventilate a given amount of air. If you quit smoking, exercise does help increase the functional capacity of the pulmonary system.

■ How can I tell if I am exceeding the safe limits for exercise participation?

The best method to determine whether you are exercising too strenuously is by checking your heart rate and making sure that it does not exceed the limits of your target zone. Exercising above the target zone may not be safe for unconditioned or high-risk individuals. Keep in mind that you do not need to exercise beyond your target zone to provide the desired benefits for the cardiovascular system.

In addition, there are several physiological signs that will tell you when you are exceeding functional limitations. A very rapid or irregular heart rate, labored breathing, nausea, vomiting, lightheadedness, headaches, dizziness, pale skin, flushness, excessive weakness, lack of energy, shakiness, sore muscles, cramps, and tightness in the chest are all signs of exercise intolerance. One of the basic things that you will need to do is learn to listen to your body. If you experience any of these signs, you should seek medical attention before continuing your exercise program.

■ How fast should heart rate decrease following aerobic exercise?

To a certain extent, recovery heart rate is related to fitness level. The higher your cardiovascular fitness level, the faster your heart rate will decrease following exercise. As a general rule of thumb, heart rate should be below 120 beats per minute five minutes into recovery. If your heart rate is above 120, you have most likely overexerted yourself or could possibly have some other cardiac abnormality. If you decrease the intensity and/or duration of exercise and you still experience a fast heart rate five minutes into recovery, you should consult a physician regarding this condition.

■ **Do people really experience a "physical high" during aerobic exercise?**

During vigorous exercise, morphine-like substances referred to as endorphines are released from the pituitary gland in the brain. These act not only as a pain killer, but can also induce feelings of euphoria and natural well-being. Increased levels of endorphines are commonly seen as a result of aerobic endurance activities and may remain elevated for as long as thirty to sixty minutes following exercise. Many experts now feel that these higher levels explain the so-called "physical high" that people experience during and after prolonged exercise participation.

Endorphine levels have also been shown to be elevated during pregnancy and delivery. Since endorphines act as pain killers, these higher levels could explain a woman's increased tolerance to the pain and discomfort experienced during natural childbirth and the pleasant feelings experienced shortly after the birth of the baby. Since several surveys have shown shorter and easier labor among well-conditioned women, it is very possible that these women may achieve higher endorphine levels during delivery, therefore, making childbirth less traumatic as compared to untrained women.

■ **How fast are the benefits of exercise lost after a person stops exercising?**

The length of time involved in losing the benefits of exercise varies among the different components of fitness and will also depend on the type of condition achieved prior to cessation. In regard to cardiovascular endurance, it has been estimated that four weeks of aerobic training are completely reversed in two consecutive weeks of physical inactivity. On the other hand, if you have been exercising regularly for months or years, two weeks of inactivity will not hurt you as much as someone who has only exercised for a few weeks. As a rule of thumb, after only forty-eight hours of aerobic inactivity, the cardiovascular system starts to lose some of its capacity. Flexibility can be maintained with two or three stretching sessions per week, and strength is easily maintained with just one maximal training session per week.

To maintain adequate fitness, it is recommended that you maintain a regular exercise program, even during periods of vacation. If you have to interrupt your program for reasons beyond your control, do not attempt to resume your training at the same level where you left off, but rather build up gradually again.

■   **What type of clothing should I wear when I exercise?**

The type of clothing to be used during exercise should fit you comfortably and allow for free movement of the different body parts. You should also select your clothes according to ambient temperature and humidity. Avoid nylon and rubberized materials and tight clothes that will interfere with the cooling mechanism of the human body and/or obstruct normal blood flow. Proper-fitting shoes, manufactured specifically for your choice of activity, are also recommended to prevent lower limb injuries.

■   **What time of the day is best for exercise?**

Just about any time of the day is fine with the exception of the noon and early afternoon hours on hot and humid days. Many people enjoy exercising early in the morning because it gives them a good boost to start the day. Others prefer the lunch hour for weight control reasons. By exercising at noon they do not eat as big a lunch, which helps keep daily caloric intake down. Highly stressed people seem to like the evening hours because of the relaxation effects of exercise.

■   **How long should a person wait after a meal before engaging in strenuous physical exercise?**

The length of time that an individual should wait before exercising after a meal depends on the amount of food consumed. On the average, after a regular meal, a person should wait about two hours before participating in strenuous physical activity. There is no reason, however, why a person should not be able to take a walk or do some other light physical activity following a meal. If anything, such practice helps burn extra calories and may help the body metabolize fats more effectively.

■   **How should acute sports injuries be treated?**

The best treatment has always been prevention itself. If a given activity is causing unusual discomfort or chronic irritation, you need to treat the cause by decreasing the intensity, switching activities, or using better equipment such as adequate and proper-fitting shoes.

If an acute injury has occurred, the standard method of treatment is cold application, compression and/or splinting, and elevation of the affected body part. Cold should be applied three to five times a day for fifteen to forty-eight minutes at a time during the first thirty-six hours. Cold can be applied by either submerging the injured area in ice-cold water, using an ice bag, or applying ice massage to the affected part. Compression can be applied with an elastic bandage or wrap. Elevation, whenever possible, is used to decrease blood flow to the injured part. The purpose of these three treatment modalities is to minimize swelling in the area, which significantly increases the time of recovery. After the initial thirty-six to forty-eight hours, heat can be used if there is no further swelling or inflammation. However, if you have doubts regarding the nature or seriousness of the injury (such as suspected fracture), you should seek a medical evaluation.

Whenever there is obvious deformity, such as in fractures, dislocations, or partial dislocations, splinting, cold application with an ice bag, and medical attention are required. Never try to reset any of these conditions by yourself, as greater damage to muscles, ligaments, and nerves is possible. The treatment of these injuries should always be left to specialized medical personnel. A quick reference guide for the signs or symptoms and treatment of exercise-related problems is provided in Table 6.1.

■ What causes muscle soreness and stiffness?

Muscle soreness and stiffness is very common among individuals who initiate an exercise program or participate after a prolonged layoff from exercise. The acute soreness experienced the first few hours after exercise is thought to be related to a lack of blood (oxygen) flow and general fatigue of the exercised muscles. The delayed soreness that appears several hours after exercise (usually twelve hours later) and lasts for two to four days may be related to actual minute tears in muscle tissue, muscle spasms that increase fluid retention stimulating the pain nerve endings, and over-stretching or tearing of connective tissue in and around muscles and joints.

The best way to prevent soreness and stiffness is by stretching adequately before and after exercise, and using a gradual progression into your exercise program. Do not attempt to do too much too quickly. If you experience soreness and stiffness, mild stretching, low-intensity exercise to stimulate blood flow, and a warm bath can help relieve the pain.

■ How should I care for shin splints?

Shin splints or pain and irritation in the shin region of the leg is a frequent sports injury encountered by participants in fitness programs.

FIGURE 6.1. Reference guide for exercise-related problems

Injury	Signs/Symptoms	Treatment*
Bruise (contusion)	Pain, swelling, discoloration	Cold application, compression, rest
Dislocations Fractures	Pain, swelling, deformity	Splinting, cold application, seek medical attention
Heat cramps	Cramps, spasms and muscle twitching in the legs, arms, and abdomen	Stop activity, get out of the heat, stretch, massage the painful area, drink plenty of fluids
Heat exhaustion	Fainting, profuse sweating, cold/clammy skin, weak/rapid pulse, weakness, headache	Stop activity, rest in a cool place, loosen clothing, rub body with cool/wet towel, drink plenty of fluids, stay out of heat for 2-3 days
Heat stroke	Hot/dry skin, no sweating, serious disorientation, rapid/full pulse, vomiting, diarrhea, unconsciousness, high body temperature	*Seek immediate medical attention*, request help and get out of the sun, bathe in cold water/spray with cold water/rub body with cold towels, drink plenty of cold fluids
Joint sprains	Pain, tenderness, swelling, loss of use, discoloration	Cold application, compression, elevation, rest, heat after 36 to 48 hours (if no further swelling)
Muscle cramps	Pain, spasm	Stretch muscle(s), use mild exercises for involved area
Muscle soreness and stiffness	Tenderness, pain	Mild stretching, low-intensity exercise, warm bath
Muscle strains	Pain, tenderness, swelling, loss of use	Cold application, compression, elevation, rest, heat after 36 to 48 hours (if no further swelling)
Shin splints	Pain, tenderness	Cold application prior to and following any physical activity, rest, heat (if no activity is carried out)
Side stitch	Pain on the side of the abdomen below the rib cage	Decrease level of physical activity or stop altogether, gradually increase level of fitness
Tendonitis	Pain, tenderness, loss of use	Rest, cold application, heat after 48 hours

* Cold should be applied 3 to 4 times a day for 15 minutes
  Heat can be applied 3 times a day for 15 to 20 minutes

Shin splints are usually the result of one or more of the following: (a) lack of proper and gradual conditioning, (b) conducting physical activities on hard surfaces (wooden floors, hard tracks, cement, and asphalt), (c) fallen arches, (d) chronic overuse, (e) muscle fatigue, (f) faulty posture, (g) inadequate shoes, and (h) being excessively overweight and participating in weight-bearing activities.

Shin splints may be managed by: (a) removing or reducing the causing agent (exercising on softer surfaces, wearing better shoes and/or archsupports, or completely stopping exercise until the shin splints heal), (b) doing mild stretching exercises before and after physical activity, (c) use of ice massage for ten to twenty minutes prior to and following physical participation, and (d) active heat (whirlpool and hot baths) for fifteen minutes, two to three times a day. In addition, supportive taping during physical activity is helpful (the proper taping technique can be easily learned from a qualified athletic trainer).

■ What causes side stitch?

The exact cause of this sharp pain that sometimes occurs during exercise is unknown. Some experts have suggested that it could be related to a lack of blood flow to the respiratory muscles during strenuous physical exertion. This stitch only seems to occur in unconditioned beginners or trained individuals when they exercise at higher intensities than usual. As you improve your physical condition, this problem will disappear unless you start training at a higher intensity. Whenever you experience this problem, you need to slow down, and if it still persists, stop altogether.

■ What causes muscle cramps, and what should be done when they occur?

Muscle cramps are caused by the body's depletion of essential electrolytes or a breakdown in the coordination between opposing muscle groups. If you have a muscle cramp, initially you should attempt to stretch the muscles involved. For example, in the case of the calf muscle, pull your toes up toward the knees. After stretching the muscles, gently rub them down, and finally do some mild exercises that require the use of those particular muscles.

In pregnant and lactating women, muscle cramps are often related to a lack of calcium. If women experience cramps during these periods, calcium supplements usually relieve the problem. Tight clothing can also cause cramps because of decreased blood flow to active muscle tissue.

■ Why is it unsafe to exercise in hot and humid conditions?

When a person exercises, only 30 to 40 percent of the energy produced in the body is used for mechanical work or movement. The rest of the energy (60 to 70 percent) is converted into heat. If this heat cannot be properly dissipated because it is either too hot or the relative humidity is too high, body temperature will increase, and in extreme cases even death can occur.

The specific heat of body tissue (the heat required to raise the temperature of the body by one degree Centigrade) is 0.38 calories per pound of body weight per one degree Centigrade (0.38 cal/lb/°C). This indicates that if no body heat is dissipated, a 150-pound person would only need to burn 57 calories (150 × 0.38) to increase total body temperature by one degree Centigrade. If this person conducted an exercise session that required 300 calories (about three miles running) without any heat dissipation, inner body temperature would increase by 5.3 degrees Centigrade, or the equivalent of going from 98.6 to 108.1 degrees Fahrenheit!

The above example clearly illustrates why caution should be used when exercising in hot or humid weather. If the relative humidity is too high, body heat cannot be lost through evaporation because the atmosphere is already saturated with water vapor. In one specific instance, a football casualty occurred at a temperature of only sixty-four degrees Fahrenheit, but at a relative humidity of 100 percent. Caution must be taken when air temperature is above ninety degrees and the relative humidity is above 60 percent.

Perhaps the best recommendation is to watch for typical heat-related symptoms. Heat exhaustion symptoms usually include cramping, weakness, headaches, dizziness, confusion, hyper-ventilation, and nausea or vomiting. If you notice any of these changes when you exercise, stop your work-out and allow yourself to recover in a cool environment, providing adequate fluid replacement.

Heat stroke symptoms include serious disorientation, warm/dry skin, rapid pulse, diarrhea, unconsciousness, and high body temperature. As your core body temperature climbs, you may feel an unexplained anxiety. The sweating mechanism usually stops before severe symptoms occur. If your temperature exceeds 106 degrees, serious neurologic injury and death may occur. Heat stroke is a true medical emergency. You should seek immediate help and get out of the sun. Cool down rapidly by bathing in cold water or have someone rub your body with cool towels. You also need to drink plenty of fluids. If a physician is unavailable, you should be taken to the emergency room.

The American College of Sports Medicine has recommended that individuals should not engage in strenuous physical activity when the readings of a wet bulb globe thermometer exceed 82.4 degrees Fahrenheit. With this type of thermometer, the wet bulb is cooled by evaporation and on dry days will show a lower temperature than the regular (dry) thermometer. On humid days, the cooling effect is less because of decreased evaporation; hence, the difference between the wet and dry readings is not as great.

■ **What precautions must be taken when exercising in the cold?**

Exercising in the cold usually does not pose a threat to the individual's health, mainly because adequate clothing for heat conservation can be worn, and exercise by itself will increase body heat production. The popular belief that exercising in cold temperatures (thirty-two degrees Fahrenheit and less) freezes the lungs is totally false because the air is properly warmed in the air passages before it ever reaches the lungs. It is not cold that poses a threat, but rather the velocity of the wind which has a great effect on the chill factor. For example, exercising at a temperature of twenty-five degrees Fahrenheit with adequate clothing is not too cold, but if the wind is blowing at twenty-five miles per hour, the chill factor reduces the actual temperature to minus five degrees Fahrenheit. This effect is even worse if you are wet and exhausted.

When exercising in the cold, it is important that you protect the face, head, hands, and feet, as they may be subject to frostbite even when the lungs are under no risk. In cold temperatures, about 30 percent of the body's heat is lost through the head's surface area if unprotected. Wearing several layers of light-weight clothing is also preferable over one single thick layer, because warm air is trapped between layers of clothes, allowing for greater heat conservation.

SPECIAL CONSIDERATIONS FOR WOMEN

■ **Physiological differences between men and women**

There are several basic differences between men and women that affect physical performance. On the average, men are about three to four inches taller and 25 to 30 pounds heavier. The average body fat in college males is about 12 to 16 percent, while in college females it is approximately 22 to 26 percent.

Maximal oxygen uptake (aerobic capacity) is about 15 to 30 percent larger in men, primarily related to a higher hemoglobin concentration (10-14 percent) and a lower body fat content in men. The higher hemoglobin concentration allows men to carry a greater amount of oxygen during exercise, which provides an advantage during aerobic events.

The quality of muscle in men and women is the same. Men, however, are stronger because they possess a greater amount of muscle mass and have a greater capacity for muscle hypertrophy (the muscle's ability to increase in size). The increased capacity for muscle hypertrophy is related to sex specific hormones. Strength differences, nevertheless, are significantly reduced when body size and composition are taken into consideration.

Men also have wider shoulders, longer extremities, and a ten percent greater bone width, except for the pelvic width. Although there are significant differences in physiological characteristics between men and women, both respond to training in a similar manner.

■ If the potential for muscle hypertrophy in women is not as great, why do so many women body builders develop such heavy musculature?

The degree of masculinity and femininity is determined by genetic inheritance and not by the amount of physical activity. Individual variations among women in hormonal secretions of androgen, estrogen, progesterone, and testosterone cause some women to have a larger-than-average build, even without any type of physical training. Because of their larger-than-average build, many of these women often participate in sports where they can use their natural physical advantage.

Additionally, in the sport of body building the athletes follow intense training routines consisting of two or more hours of constant weight lifting with very short rest intervals between sets. Many times during the training routine, back-to-back exercises that require the use of the same muscle groups are performed. The objective of this type of training is to "pump" extra blood into the muscles, which makes the muscles appear much bigger than they really are in resting conditions. Based on the intensity and the length of the training session, the muscles can remain filled with blood, appearing measurably larger for several hours after completing the training session. Therefore, in real life, these women are not as muscular as they seem when they are "pumped up" for a contest.

In the sport of body building, a big point of controversy is the use of anabolic steroids and human growth hormones, even among women participants. Anabolic steroids are synthetic versions of the male sex hormone testosterone, which promotes muscle development and hypertrophy. The use of these hormones, however, can produce detrimental and undesirable side effects, which some women deem tolerable (e.g., hypertension, fluid retention, decreased breast size, deepening of the voice, facial whiskers, and body hair growth). The use of these steroids among women is definitely on the increase, and according to several sports-medicine physicians, about 80 percent of women body builders have used steroids. Furthermore, several women's track-and-field coaches have indicated that as many as 95 percent of women athletes around the world in this sport will use anabolic steroids in order to remain competitive at the international level.

There is no doubt that women who take steroids will indeed build heavy musculature like men, and if taken long enough, will lead to masculinizing effects in all women. As a result, the International Federation of Body Building recently instituted a mandatory steroid-testing program among women participating in the Miss Olympia contest. When drugs are not used to promote development, increased health and femininity are the rule rather than the exception among women who participate in body building, strength training, or sports in general.

■ Does exercise participation hinder menstruation?

Although, on the average, women experience a decrease in physical capacity during menstruation, medical surveys at the Olympic Games have shown that women have broken Olympic and world records at all stages of the menstrual cycle. Menstruation should not keep a woman from participating in athletics, nor will it necessarily have a negative impact on performance.

In some instances, highly trained athletes may develop amenorrhea (cessation of menstruation) or oligomenorrhea (irregular menstruation) during training and competition. This condition is primarily seen in extremely lean athletes who also engage in sports that require very strenuous physical effort over a sustained period of time, but it is by no means irreversible. At present, it is unknown whether the condition is caused by physical and/or emotional stress related to high-intensity training; excessively low body fat; or other such factors as decreased ovarian function, increased testosterone levels, or changes in hypothalamic function.

■ Does exercise help relieve dysmenorrhea (painful menstruation)?

Exercise has not been shown to either cure or aggravate painful menstruation, but it has been shown to relieve menstrual cramps because of improved circulation to the uterus. The decrease in menstrual cramps could also be related to increased levels of endorphines produced during prolonged physical activity that may counteract pain.

■ **Is it safe to exercise during pregnancy?**

There is no reason why women should not exercise during pregnancy. If anything, it is desirable that women do so to strengthen the body and prepare for delivery. Some survey results have shown that physically fit women experience shorter labor, easier delivery, and faster recovery as compared to unfit women.

Among Indian tribes it is commonly observed that pregnant women continue to carry out all of their hard labor chores up to the very day of delivery, and a few hours after the birth of the baby they resume their normal activities. There have also been several women athletes who have competed in different sports during the early stages of pregnancy. At the 1952 Olympic Games, a bronze medal in track and field was won by a pregnant woman. Nevertheless, the final decision for exercise participation should be made between the woman and her personal physician.

Many experts in this area have recommended that if a woman has been exercising regularly, similar activities can be carried out through the fifth month of pregnancy, but they should take care not to exceed a working heart rate of 140 beats per minute. Activities conducted at higher exercise intensities may decrease the available oxygen in the circulatory system and can lead to increases in body temperature of the mother and the fetus. After the fifth month, walking and/or moderate swimming are indicated in conjunction with some light strengthening exercises. For women who have not exercised regularly, fifteen minutes of daily walking and light strengthening exercises are recommended throughout the entire pregnancy.

■ **What is osteoporosis and how can it be prevented?**

Osteoporosis has been defined as the softening, deterioration, or loss of total body bone. Bones become so weak and brittle that fractures, primarily of the hip, wrist, and spine, occur very readily. About 1.3 million fractures are attributed to this condition each year. Osteoporosis slowly begins in the third and fourth decade of life, and women are especially susceptible after menopause. This is primarily due to estrogen loss following menopause, which increases the rate at which bone mass is broken down.

The prevention of osteoporosis begins early in life by providing adequate amounts of calcium in the diet (follow the recommended dietary allowance of 800 to 1,200 mg per day) and regularly participating in an exercise program. Weight-bearing activities such as walking, jogging, and weight training are especially helpful, because not only do they tone up muscles, but also develop stronger and thicker bones.

Following menopause, daily calcium intake should be in the range of 1,000 to 1,500 mg per day. Adequate physical exercise and personal evaluation by your physician for possible estrogen therapy and calcium supplements are also recommended to prevent osteoporosis. In conjunction with adequate calcium intake, there may be a need for an additional amount of vitamin D, which is necessary for optimal calcium absorption. For your information, a list of selected foods and their respective calcium content is provided in Table 6.2.

TABLE 6.2. Lowfat calcium-rich foods.

Food	Amount	Calcium (mg)	Calories	Calories from Fat
Beans, red kidney, cooked	1 cup	70	218	4%
Beet, greens, cooked	1/2 cup	72	13	—
Broccoli, cooked, drained	1 sm stalk	123	36	—
Burrito, bean	1	173	307	28%
Cottage cheese, 2% lowfat	1/2 cup	78	103	18%
Milk, nonfat, powdered	1 tbsp	52	27	1%
Milk, skim	1 cup	296	88	3%
Ice milk (vanilla)	1/2 cup	102	100	27%
Instant breakfast, whole milk	1 cup	301	280	26%
Kale, cooked, drained	1/2 cup	103	22	—
Okra, cooked, drained	1/2 cup	74	23	—
Shrimp, boiled	3 oz.	99	99	9%
Spinach, raw	1 cup	51	14	—
Yogurt, fruit	1 cup	345	231	8%
Yogurt, lowfat, plain	1 cup	271	160	20%

■ **Do women have special iron needs?**

The recommended dietary allowance of iron for women is 18 mg per day (10 mg for men). Unfortunately, it is estimated that 30 to 50 percent of child-bearing age women in the United States have an iron deficiency. People who do not have an adequate iron intake can develop iron deficiency anemia, a condition in which the concentration of hemoglobin in the red blood cells is reduced.

Some researchers have indicated that physically active women may also have a higher than average iron need. It is thought that heavy training creates an iron demand higher than the recommended intake because small amounts of iron are lost through sweat, urine, and stools. Mechanical trauma, caused by the pounding of the feet on pavement during extensive jogging, may also lead to the destruction of iron-containing red blood cells. A large percentage of endurance female athletes have been reported to suffer from iron deficiency. Blood ferritin levels, a measure of stored iron in the human body, should be checked frequently in women who participate in intense physical training.

There are also some individuals who have higher rates of iron absorption or faster rates of iron loss. In most cases, nonetheless, adequate iron intake can be achieved by eating more iron-rich foods such as beans, peas, green leafy vegetables, enriched grain products, egg yolk, fish, and lean meats (organ meats are especially good sources, but they are also high in cholesterol). A list of foods high in iron content is given in Table 6.3.

TABLE 6.3. Iron-rich foods.

Food	Amount	Iron (mg)	Calories	Choles-terol	Calories from Fat
Beans, red kidney, cooked	1 cup	4.4	218	0	4%
Beef, ground lean	3 oz.	3.0	186	81	48%
Beef, sirloin	3 oz.	2.5	329	77	74%
Beef, liver, fried	3 oz.	7.5	195	345	42%
Beet, greens, cooked	1/2 cup	1.4	13	0	—
Broccoli, cooked, drained	1 sm stalk	1.1	36	0	—
Burrito, bean	1	2.4	307	14	28%
Egg, hard, cooked	1	1.0	72	250	63%
Farina (Cream of Wheat), cooked	1/2 cup	6.0	51	0	—
Instant breakfast, whole milk	1 cup	8.0	280	33	26%
Peas, frozen, cooked, drained	1/2 cup	1.5	55	0	—
Shrimp, boiled	3 oz.	2.7	99	128	9%
Spinach, raw	1 cup	1.7	14	0	—
Vegetables, mixed, cooked	1 cup	2.4	116	0	—

NUTRITION AND WEIGHT CONTROL QUESTIONS

■ What is the difference between a calorie and a kilocalorie (kcal)?

A calorie is a unit of measure used to indicate the energy value of food and cost of physical activity. Technically, a kcal or large calorie is the amount of heat necessary to raise the temperature of one kilogram of water from 14.5 to 15.5 degrees Centigrade, but for the purpose of simplicity, people refer to it as a calorie rather than kcal. For example, if the caloric value of a given food is 100 calories (kcal), the energy contained in this food could raise the temperature of 100 kilograms of water by one degree Centigrade.

■ Does cooking affect the amount of calories contained in food?

Cooking does not significantly alter the caloric content of food. The only exception would be meat, where broiling and barbecuing drains off some of the fat and decreases the caloric content. On the other hand, frying will significantly increase the caloric content of food.

■ Why do some people gain weight rather than lose weight when they initiate an exercise program?

Physical exercise leads to an increase in lean body mass. Therefore, it is not uncommon for body weight to remain the same or increase when you initiate an exercise program, while inches and percent body fat decrease. The increase in lean tissue results in an increased functional capacity of the human body. With exercise, most of the weight (fat) loss is seen after a few weeks of training, when the lean component has stabilized.

"Skinny" people should also realize that the only healthy manner to increase body weight is through exercise, primarily strength-training exercises. Attempting to gain weight by just overeating will increase the fat component and not the lean component, which is not conducive to better health. Consequently, exercise is the best solution to weight (fat) reduction as well as weight (lean) gain.

■ Are rubberized sweatsuits and steam baths an effective way to lose weight?

The answer to this question is simply no! If you use a sweatsuit or step into a sauna, there is a significant amount of water loss but not fat. Sure, it looks nice immediately after when you step on the scale, but it is just a false loss of weight. As soon as you replace body fluids, the weight is quickly gained back. Wearing rubberized sweatsuits not only increases the rate of body fluid loss, which is vital during prolonged exercise, but also increases core temperature. Dehydration through these methods leads to impaired cellular function and in extreme cases even death.

■ Can cellulite be decreased with special exercises?

There is no such thing as cellulite. Some people use the term cellulite in reference to fat deposits that "bulge out." Cellulite, however, is nothing but excessive accumulation of body fat.

The reader needs to realize that there is no such thing as spot reducing. Since the body draws its energy from all fat stores simultaneously, and not just the parts exercised, there are no special exercises that will help decrease fat in a specific body area. Nevertheless, if you engage in long-duration aerobic exercise, a greater proportion of fat can be drawn from the larger fat stores because of the high caloric requirement of the activity.

The only effective way to decrease body fat is through a combined lifetime food selection modification program and a regular exercise program. You will need willpower, patience, and persistence. If you really try, it will work. The best tip, though, is to keep the weight (fat) off, rather than let it go and try to control it once it has crept up on you. Keep in mind that only one person in 100 is able to keep the weight off after a successful weight loss program. The very few who succeed are those who implement lifetime changes in food selection and physical activity habits. As more people become educated and apply these two basic principles, the rate of success will increase.

■ Are mechanical vibrators useful in losing weight?

Some people will go to extremes in order to lose weight and still overindulge in food consumption. Such individuals can be easily deceived and often resort to the "quick fix" in an attempt to solve their weight problem. Mechanical vibrators are worthless in a weight control program. Vibrating belts and turning rollers may feel good but require no effort whatsoever on the part of the muscles. Fat can not be "shaken off" it has to be burned off in muscle tissue.

■ How detrimental are coffee and alcohol to good health?

Caffeine and alcohol are drugs, and as such can produce several undesirable side effects. Caffeine doses in excess of 200 to 500 mg can produce an abnormally rapid heart rate, abnormal heart rhythms, increased blood pressure, birth defects, and increased body temperature. They can induce symptoms of anxiety, depression, nervousness, and dizziness, as well as increased secretion of gastric acids leading to stomach problems. The caffeine content of different drinks varies depending upon the product. For six ounces of coffee, the content varies from 65 mg for instant coffee to as high as 180 mg for drip coffee. Soft drinks, mainly colas, range in caffeine content from 30 mg to 60 mg per twelve-ounce can.

Among the detrimental effects caused by alcohol are liver damage (cirrhosis of the liver is among the fastest rising causes of death in the country), increased risk for accidents, increased nutritional deficiencies, increased serum triglycerides, obesity, a disturbance in carbohydrate metabolism, a decreased ability to use oxygen at the muscular level, and an increased risk of birth defects during pregnancy. Forty percent of the people in the United States will be involved in alcohol-related car accidents at some point in their lifetime. Drinking during pregnancy is rated among the top three causes leading to birth defects, and it is the only one that is completely preventable. One of the most significant ill effects of alcoholism, however, is the breakdown of the family unit; which has an effect on the physical, emotional, and spiritual well-being of the person. Unfortunately, many times people start out as occasional social drinkers, and before they realize it, they have turned into alcoholics and are not willing to accept this fact.

The negative effects of long-term caffeine and alcohol consumption, even in moderate amounts, are probably more detrimental to health and well-being than any short-term benefits derived from their consumption.

■ **Do athletes or individuals who train for long periods of time need a special diet?**

Many people have felt that highly trained individuals need a special diet in order to be successful in their sport. The simple truth is that unless the diet is deficient in basic nutrients, there are no special, secret, or magic diets that will help a person perform better or develop faster as a result of what they are eating. Athletes' diets do not have to be any different from the regular recommended diet (60 percent carbohydrates, less than 30 percent fat, and about 15 to 20 percent protein). As long as the diet is balanced, that is, it meets the daily servings from each of the four food groups, athletes do not need any additional supplements. Even in strength training and body building no additional protein in excess of 20 percent of the total daily caloric intake is needed.

The only difference between a sedentary person and a highly trained one is in the total number of calories required on a daily basis. The trained person may consume more calories because of the increased energy expenditure as a result of intense physical training.

The only time a normal diet should be modified is when an individual is going to participate in long-distance events lasting in excess of one hour (e.g., marathon, triathlon, and road cycling). Athletic performance is increased for these types of events by consuming a diet high in carbohydrates (about 70 percent) along with a progressive decrease in training intensity the last three days before the event.

■   **What are the recommended guidelines for fluid replacement during prolonged aerobic exercise?**

The main objective of fluid replacement during prolonged aerobic exercise is to maintain the blood volume so that circulation and sweating can continue at normal levels. Adequate water replacement is the most important factor in the prevention of heat disorders. Drinking about eight ounces of cool water every ten to fifteen minutes during exercise seems to be ideal to prevent dehydration. Cold fluids seem to be absorbed more rapidly from the stomach.

Commercial fluid replacement solutions (e.g., Take-Five, Gatorade) contain about five percent glucose, which slows down water absorbtion during exercise in the heat. During prolonged aerobic exercise in cool environments, commercially prepared solutions may be advantageous because not as much water is lost through the sweating mechanism. Be aware that it takes about 30 minutes for sugar to become available to the muscles following ingestion of a glucose solution. Drinking solutions with a sugar concentration higher than five percent will significantly retard water absorption from the stomach.

EXERCISE AND AGING

Exercise programs for older adults

Unlike any previous time in American society, the elderly constitute the fastest growing segment of our population. In 1880, less than three percent of the total population, or fewer than two million people, were over the age of 65. By 1980, the elderly population had reached approximately 25 million, representing over 11.3 percent of the population. It has been estimated that the elderly will make up more than 20 percent of the total population by the year 2035.

Historically, the elderly population has been neglected in the development of fitness programs. Adequate fitness is just as important for older individuals as it is for young people. While much research remains to be done in this area, studies indicate that older individuals who are physically fit also enjoy better health and a higher quality of life.

The main objective of fitness programs for older adults should be to improve the functional capacity of the participant. A committee of the American Alliance of Health, Physical Education, Recreation, and Dance (AAHPERD) recently defined functional fitness for older adults as "the physical capacity of the individual to meet ordinary and unexpected demands of daily life safely and effectively." This definition clearly indicates the need for fitness programs that closely relate to activities normally encountered by this population. The AAHPERD committee encourages participation in programs that will help develop cardio-vascular endurance, localized muscular endurance, muscular flexibility, agility and balance, and motor coordination. A copy of a recently developed battery of fitness tests for older adults can be obtained from the AAHPERD national office in Reston, Virginia.

■ **What is the relationship between aging and physical work capacity?**

While previous research studies have documented declines in physio-logical functioning and motor capacity as a result of aging, at present there is no hard evidence which proves that declines in physical work capacity are mainly related to the aging process. Lack of physical activity, a common phenomena seen in our society as people age, may cause decreases in physical work capacity that are by far greater than the effects of aging itself. Some of the earlier studies in this area had shown a 10 to 15 percent decline in endurance per decade of life. Relatively recent research, however, has shown a decline of only about five percent.

Data on individuals who have engaged in systematic physical activity throughout life indicate that these groups of people maintain a higher level of functional capacity and do not experience the typical declines in later years. Dr. George Sheehan, cardiologist and runner, states that, from a func-tional point of view, the typical American is 30 years older than his/her chronological age indicates. In other words, an active sixty-year-old person can have a similar work capacity as a sedentary thirty-year-old individual.

■ **Do older adults respond to physical training?**

The trainability of both elderly men and women and the effectiveness of physical activity as a relative modality has been demonstrated in prior research. Older adults who increase their level of physical activity will experience significant changes in cardiovascular endurance, strength, and flexibility. The extent of the changes depends on their initial fitness level and the types of activities selected for their training (walking, cycling, strength training, etc.).

Data on maximal oxygen uptake values has shown that the average decline with aging is approximately 0.4 ml/kg/min per year. In active indi-viduals, however, the decline is only about 0.2 ml/kg/min. In regard to strength development, research has shown that although older adults can significantly increase their strength levels, the amount of muscle hyper-trophy achieved decreases with age. In terms of body composition, after the age of 60, inactive adults continue to gain body fat despite the fact that body weight tends to decrease.

Older adults who wish to initiate or continue an exercise program are strongly encouraged to have a complete medical exam, including a stress electrocardiogram test (see Chapter 5, pages 148-149). Recommended activities for older adults include calisthenics, walking, jogging, swimming, cycling, and water aerobics. Isometric and other intense weight training exercises should be avoided. Activities that require an all-out effort and/or require participants to hold their breath (valsalva maneuver) tend to decrease blood flow to the heart and cause a significant increase in blood pressure and the load placed on the heart. Older adults should participate in activities that require continuous and rhythmic muscular activity (about 50 to 70 percent of functional capacity). Such activities do not cause large increases in blood pressure or place an intense overload on the heart.

WHAT IS NEXT NOW THAT I HAVE COMPLETED THE ASSIGNMENTS IN THIS BOOK?

The objective of this book was to provide you with the information necessary to implement your personal fitness and wellness program. If you have read and successfully completed your assignments, including a regular exercise program, you should be convinced of the value of exercise and healthy lifestyle habits in the achievement of total well-being.

The real challenge will come now that you are about to finish this course: a lifetime commitment to fitness and wellness. It is a lot easier to adhere to the program while in a structured setting. Nonetheless, as you continue with your personal program, keep in mind that the greatest benefit of fitness and wellness is to improve the quality of your life.

For most people who engage in a personal fitness and wellness program, this new quality of life is experienced after only a few weeks of training and practicing healthy lifestyle patterns. In some instances, especially for individuals who have led a poor lifestyle for a long time, it may take a few months before positive habits are established and feelings of well-being are experienced. But in the end, everyone who applies the principles of fitness and wellness will reap the desired benefits. Being diligent and taking control of yourself will provide you with a better, happier, healthier, and more productive life. And once you get there, you will not want to have it any other way.

References

1. Allsen, P. E., J. M. Harrison, and B. Vance. *Fitness for Life: An Individualized Approach.* Dubuque, IA: Wm. C. Brown, 1989.

2. American Heart Association. *1988 Heart Facts.* Dallas, TX: The Association, 1988.

3. American College of Sports Medicine. *Guidelines for Exercise Testing and Prescription.* Philadelphia: Lea and Febiger, 1986.

4. American Cancer Society. *1988 Cancer Facts and Figures.* New York: The Society, 1988.

5. Bennett, W., and J. Gurin. "Do Diets Really Work?" *Science* 42-50, March 1982.

6. Christian, J. L. and J. L. Greger. *Nutrition for Living.* Menlo Park, CA: The Benjamin/Cummings Publishing Company, Inc., 1988.

7. Cooper, K. H. *The Aerobics Program for Total Well-Being.* New York: Mount Evans and Co., 1982.

8. Hoeger, W. W. K. *Lifetime Physical Fitness & Wellness: A Personalized Program.* Englewood, CO: Morton Publishing Company, 1989.

9. Hoeger, W. W. K. *Principles and Laboratories for Physical Fitness & Wellness.* Englewood, CO: Morton Publishing Company, 1988.

10. Jackson, A. S., M. L. Pollock, and A. Ward. "Generalized Equations for Predicting Body Density of Women." *Medicine and Science in Sports and Exercise* 3:175-182, 1980.

11. Jackson, A. S., and M. L. Pollock. "Generalized Equations for Predicting Body Density of Men." *British Journal of Nutrition* 40:497-504, 1978.

12. Karvonen, M. J., E Kentala, and O. Mustala. "The Effects of Training on the Heart Rate, a Longitudinal Study." *Annales Medicinae Experimentalis et Biologiae Fenniae* 35:307-315, 1957.

13. Morgan, B. L. G. *The Lifelong Nutrition Guide.* Englewood Cliffs, NJ: Prentice-Hall, 1983.

14. Remington, D., A. G. Fisher, and E. A. Parent. *How to Lower Your Fat Thermostat.* Provo, UT: Vitality House International, Inc. 1983.

15. Siri, W.E. *Body Composition from Fluid Spaces and Density.* Berkeley, CA: Donner Laboratory of Medical Physics, University of California, 19 March 1956.

16. *The Fallacies of Taking Supplementation.* Tufts University Diet & Nutrition Letter. July 1987.

17. Whitney, E. N. and E. V. N. Hamilton. *Understanding Nutrition.* St. Paul, MN: West Publishing Co., 1987.

18. Wiley, J. A. and T. C. Camacho. "Lifestyle and Future Health: Evidence from the Alameda County Study." *Preventive Medicine* 9:1-21, 1980.

19. Wilmore, J. H. *Training for Sport and Activity.* Boston: Allyn and Bacon, Inc., 1988.

20. *Your Back and How to Care For It.* Kenilworth, NJ: Schering Corporation, 1965.

Pre- and Post-Fitness Profiles

Date: _____ Course: _____ Section: _____

Name: _____ Age: _____ Male or Female: M/F

Body Weight: _____ . _____

Fitness Component	Test Results	Fitness Standard	Fitness Classification
Cardiovascular Endurance	Time ___.___	VO₂ max. ___.___	_____
Muscular Strength/Endurance	Reps	% tile	
Bench-Jumps 48 30 80%/9 30	_____	40%	_____
Chair-Dips/Mod. Push-Ups	30	50%	_____
Abdominal Curl-Ups 50 40/ 80% 40	_____	45%	_____
Average Percentile	_____	_____	_____
Muscular Flexibility	Inches	% tile	
Modified Sit-and-Reach 2\15 8 80%	18	60%	_____
Body Rotation (R/L)	_____	_____	_____
Average Percentile	_____	_____	_____
Body Composition	mm		
Chest/Triceps	_____ 20		
Abdominal/Suprailium	_____		
Thigh	_____	% Fat	
Sum of Skinfolds	_____	_____	120/80 109/65

Figure A.1. Personal Fitness Profile: Pre-Test

Date: _____ Course: _____ Section: _____

Name: _____ Age: _____ Male or Female: M/F

Body Weight: _____ . _____

Fitness Component	Test Results	Fitness Standard	Fitness Classification
	Time	VO$_2$ max.	
Cardiovascular Endurance	____.____	____.____	_____
Muscular Strength/Endurance	Reps	% tile	
Bench-Jumps	_____	_____	_____
Chair-Dips/Mod. Push-Ups	_____	_____	_____
Abdominal Curl-Ups	_____	_____	_____
Average Percentile		_____	_____
Muscular Flexibility	Inches	% tile	
Modified Sit-and-Reach	_____	_____	_____
Body Rotation (R/L)	R=10 L=13	_____	_____
Average Percentile		_____	_____
Body Composition	mm		
Chest/Triceps	_____		
Abdominal/Suprailium	_____		
Thigh	_____	% Fat	
Sum of Skinfolds	_____	_____	_____

Figure A.2. Personal Fitness Profile: Post-Test

PHYSICAL FITNESS PROFILE
by Sharon A. Hoeger and Werner W.K. Hoeger
Morton Publishing Company

John Doe   Age: 18

Test Item	Most Recent Test 01-15-1990	Current Test 04-18-1990	Current Fitness Rating	Percent Change
Cardiovascular Endurance (1.5-mile run test)	38.6 ml/kg/min	47.4 ml/kg/min	Good	+23
Muscular Strength and Endurance	37 %tile	58 %tile	Average	
Lat pull down	8 reps - 30 %tile	12 reps - 60 %tile	Good	+50
Leg extension	12 reps - 50 %tile	17 reps - 80 %tile	Excellent	+42
Bench press	6 reps - 30 %tile	10 reps - 50 %tile	Average	+67
Sit-up	8 reps - 40 %tile	14 reps - 70 %tile	Good	+75
Leg curl	4 reps - 20 %tile	7 reps - 30 %tile	Fair	+75
Arm curl	9 reps - 50 %tile	11 reps - 60 %tile	Good	+22
Muscular Flexibility	40 %tile	57 %tile	Average	
Sit and reach	14.5 in - 50 %tile	14.0 in - 40 %tile	Average	-3
Right body rotation	16.0 in - 30 %tile	19.0 in - 60 %tile	Good	+19
Shoulder rotation	25.0 in - 40 %tile	20.0 in - 70 %tile	Good	-20
Body Composition				
Percent body fat	22.1 %	16.6 %	Good	-25
Recommended percent body fat		12.0 %		
Body weight	168.0 lbs	154.0 lbs		
Recommended body weight		146.0 lbs		

Computer software available through Morton Publishing Company, Englewood, Colorado.

FIGURE A.3. Computerized fitness profile: pre- and post-assessment comparison.

Caloric, Protein, Fat, Saturated Fat, Cholesterol, and Carbohydrate Content of Selected Foods*

Code	Food	Amount	Weight gm	Calo- ries	Pro- tein gm	Fat gm	Sat. Fat gm	Cho- les- terol mg	Car- bohy- drate gm
001.	All-Bran cereal	1/4 c	21	53	3.0	.4	0.1	0	16
002.	Almond Joy, candy bar	1.5 oz.	42	227	2.5	12	10.2	0	28
003.	Almonds, shelled	1/4 c	36	213	6.6	19	1.4	0	9
004.	Apple, raw, unpared	1 med	150	80	0.3	1	0.0	0	20
005.	Apple juice, canned or bottled	1/2 c	124	59	0.1	0	0.0	0	15
006.	Apple pie	1 piece (3½")	118	302	2.6	13	3.5	120	45
007.	Applesauce, canned, sweetened	1/2 c	128	116	0.3	0	0.0	0	31
008.	Apricots, raw	3 (12 per lb)	114	55	1.1	0	0.0	0	14
009.	Apricots, canned, heavy syrup	3 halves; 1¾ tbsp liq.	85	73	0.5	0	0.0	0	19
010.	Apricots, dried, sulfured, uncooked	10 med halves	35	91	1.8	0	0.0	0	23
011.	Asparagus, cooked green spears	4 med	60	12	1.3	0	0.0	0	2
012.	Avocado, raw	1/2 med	120	185	2.4	19	3.2	0	7
013.	Bacon, cooked, drained	2 slices	15	86	3.8	8	2.7	30	1
014.	Bacon/lettuce/tomato sandwich	1	130	327	11.6	19	4.7	21	31
015.	Banana, nut bread	1 slice	50	169	3.0	8	1.5	33	22
016.	Banana, raw	1 sm (7¼")	140	81	1.0	0	0.0	0	21
017.	Beans, green snap, cooked	1/2 c	65	16	1.0	0	0.0	0	3
018.	Beans, lentils	1/4 c	50	53	3.9	0	0.0	0	10
019.	Beans, lima (Fordhook), froz., cooked	1/2 c	85	84	6.0	0	0.0	0	17
020.	Beans, red kidney, cooked	1 c	185	218	14.4	1	0.0	0	40
021.	Beans, refried	1/2 c	145	148	9.0	1	0.2	0	25

* Reproduced with permission from Hoeger, W. W. K. *Lifetime Physical Fitness & Wellness: A Personalized Program.* Morton Publishing Company, 1989.

Code	Food	Amount	Weight gm	Calo- ries	Pro- tein gm	Fat gm	Sat. Fat gm	Cho- les- terol mg	Car- bohy- drate gm
022.	Bean sprouts, mung, raw	1/2 c	52	18	2.0	0	0.0	0	4
023.	Beef-chuck, cooked,	3 oz.	85	212	25.0	12	7.8	80	0
024.	Beef, corned canned	3 oz.	85	163	21.0	10	8.0	70	0
025.	Beef, ground, lean	3 oz.	85	186	23.3	10	5.0	81	0
026.	Beef, meatloaf	1 piece	111	246	20.0	15	6.1	125	5.6
027.	Beef, round steak, cooked, trimmed	3 oz.	85	222	24.3	13	6.0	77	0
028.	Beef, rump roast	3 oz.	85	177	24.7	9	4.0	80	0
029.	Beef, sirloin, cooked	3 oz.	85	329	19.6	27	13.0	77	0
030.	Beef, T-bone steak	3 oz.	85	401	16.7	37	15.6	66	0
031.	Beef, thin/sliced	3 oz.	85	105	18.5	3	1.1	36	0
032.	Beer	12 fl. oz.	360	151	1.1	0	0.0	0	14
033.	Beets, red, canned, drained	1/2 c	80	32	0.8	0	0.0	0	8
034.	Beet greens, cooked	1/2 c	73	13	1.3	0	0.0	0	2
035.	Biscuits, baking powder, made from mix	1 med	35	114	2.5	6	1.1	0	18
036.	Blueberries, fresh cultivated	1/2 c	73	45	0.5	0	0.0	0	11
037.	Blueberry pie	1 piece (3½")	158	380	4.0	17	4.0	0	55
038.	Bologna	1 slice (1 oz.)	28	86	3.4	8	3.0	15	0
039.	Bouillon, broth	1 cube	4	5	.8	0	0.0	0	0
040.	Bran Cereal	1/2 c	30	72	3.8	1	0.0	0	22
041.	Brandy	1 oz.	28	69	0.0	0	0.0	0	11
042.	Bread, Corn	1 slice	78	161	5.8	6	0.1	0	23
043.	Bread, cracked wheat	1 slice	25	65	2.3	1	0.2	0	12
044.	Bread, French enriched	1 slice	35	102	3.2	1	0.2	0	19
045.	Bread, rye (American)	1 slice	25	61	2.3	0	0.0	0	13
046.	Bread, white enriched	1 slice	25	68	2.2	1	0.2	0	13
047.	Bread, whole wheat	1 slice	25	61	2.6	1	0.6	0	12
048.	Broccoli, raw	1 sm stalk	114	38	4.1	0	0.0	0	7
049.	Broccoli, cooked drained	1 sm stalk	140	36	4.3	0	0.0	0	6
050.	Brownies, with nuts	1	20	95	1.3	6	1.4	18	11
051.	Brussels sprouts, froz., cooked drained	1/2 c	78	28	3.2	0	0.0	0	5
052.	Bulgur, wheat	1 c	135	227	8.4	1	0.0	0	47
053.	Burrito, bean	1	166	307	12.5	9.5	3.6	14	48
054.	Burrito, combination, Taco Bell	1	175	404	21.0	16	0.0	0	43
055.	Butter	1 tsp	5	36	0.0	4	0.4	12	0
056.	Buttermilk, cultured	1 c	245	88	8.8	0	1.3	5	12
057.	Cabbage, raw chopped	1/2 c	45	11	0.6	0	0.0	0	3
058.	Cabbage, boiled, drained wedge	1/2 c	85	16	0.9	0	0.0	0	3
059.	Cake, angel food, plain	1 piece	60	161	4.3	0	0.0	0	36
060.	Cake, devil's food, iced	1 piece	99	365	4.5	16	5.0	68	55
061.	Candy, hard	1 oz.	28	109	0.0	0	0.0	0	28
062.	Cantaloupe	1/4 melon 5" diam.	239	35	2.0	0	0.0	0	10
063.	Caramel (candy, plain or choc.)	1 oz.	28	113	1.1	3	1.6	0	22
064.	Carrots, raw	1 carrot 7½" long	81	30	0.8	0	0.0	0	7
065.	Carrots, cooked, drained	1/2 c	73	23	0.7	0	0.0	0	5
066.	Cashew-roasted-unsalted	2 oz.	57	326	9.2	27	5.4	0	16
067.	Cauliflower, cooked, drained	1/2 c	63	14	1.5	0	0.0	0	3

Code	Food	Amount	Weight gm	Calo- ries	Pro- tein gm	Fat gm	Sat. Fat gm	Cho- les- terol mg	Car- bohy- drate gm
068.	Celery, green, raw, long	1 outer stalk 8"	40	7	0.4	0	0.0	0	2
069.	Champagne	4 oz.	113	87	0.2	0	0.0	0	2
070.	Cheerios cereal	1 c	23	89	3.4	1	0.2	0	16
071.	Cheese, American	1 oz. slice	28	100	6.0	8	5.6	17	0
072.	Cheese, blue	1 oz.	28	100	6.0	8	5.3	25	1
073.	Cheese, cheddar	1 oz.	28	114	7.0	9	6.0	30	0
074.	Cheese, cottage, 2%	1/2 c	113	103	15.5	2	1.4	10	44
075.	Cheese, cottage, creamed	1/2 cup	105	112	14.0	5	6.4	15	3
076.	Cheese, creamed	1 oz.	28	99	6.0	8	3.0	31	1
077.	Cheese, souffle	1 portion	110	240	10.9	19	9.5	189	7
078.	Cheeseburger, McDonalds	1	115	321	15.2	16	6.7	40	29
079.	Cheesecake	1 piece (3½")	85	257	4.6	16	9.0	150	24
080.	Cherries	10	75	47	0.9	0	0.0	0	12
081.	Cherry Pie	1 piece (3½")	118	308	3.1	13	5.0	137	45
082.	Chicken breast/roast w/skin	1	98	193	29.2	8	2.1	83	0
083.	Chicken, drumstick Kentucky Fried	1	54	136	14.0	8	2.2	73	2
084.	Chicken, drumstick, roasted	1	52	112	14.1	6	1.6	48	0
085.	Chicken McNuggets	6	111	329	19.5	21	5.2	64	15
086.	Chicken, patty sandwich	1	157	436	24.8	23	6.1	68	34
087.	Chicken, wing, Kentucky Fried	1	45	151	11.0	10	2.9	70	4
088.	Chicken, roast, light meat without skin	3 oz.	85	141	27.0	3	0.4	45	0
089.	Chicken, roast, dark meat without skin	3 oz.	85	149	24.0	5	0.8	50	0
090.	Chili con carne	1 c	255	339	19.1	16	5.8	28	31
091.	Chocolate cake w/icing	1 piece	69	235	3.0	8	3.6	37	40
092.	Chocolate fudge	1 oz.	28	115	0.6	3	2.1	1	21
093.	Chocolate, M&M's, plain	1 oz.	28	140	1.9	6	3.3	0	19
094.	Chocolate, M&M's w/peanuts	1 oz.	28	145	3.2	7	3.2	0	16
095.	Chocolate, milk	1 oz.	28	147	2.0	9	3.6	5	16
096.	Chocolate, milk w/almonds	1 oz.	28	150	2.9	10	4.4	5	15
097.	Chocolate, Milky way bar	1 oz.	28	128	1.4	4	3.0	7	20
098.	Chocolate, Snickers bar	1 oz.	28	138	3.0	6	3.0	0	17
099.	Clam, canned drained	3 oz.	85	83	13.0	2	0.2	50	2
100.	Clam chowder (north east)	1 c	248	163	9.5	7	3.0	22	16
101.	Cocoa, hot, with whole milk	1 c	250	218	9.1	9	6.1	33	26
102.	Cocoa, plain, dry	1 tbsp	5	14	0.9	1	0.0	0	3
103.	Coconut, shredded, packed	1/2 c	65	225	2.3	23	20.0	0	6
104.	Cod, cooked	3 oz.	85	144	24.3	4	1.5	60	0
105.	Coffee	3/4 cup	180	1	0.0	0	0.0	0	0
106.	Coffee cake	1 piece	72	230	4.5	7	2.5	47	38
107.	Cola	12 oz.	369	144	0.0	0	0.0	0	37
108.	Coleslaw	1 c	120	173	1.6	17	1.0	5	6
109.	Collards, leaves without stems, cooked, drained	1/2 c	95	32	3.4	1	2.0	0	5
110.	Cookies, chocolate chip homemade	2 2¼" diam.	20	103	1.0	6	1.7	14	12
111.	Cookies, oatmeal raisin	2 2" diam.	26	122	1.5	5	1.3	1	18
112.	Cookies, vanilla	5 1¾" diam.	20	93	1.0	3	0.8	10	15
113.	Corn, boiled on cob	1 ear 5" long	140	70	2.5	1	0.0	0	16
114.	Corn, canned, drained	1/2 c	83	70	2.2	1	0.0	0	16

Code	Food	Amount	Weight gm	Calo- ries	Pro- tein gm	Fat gm	Sat. Fat gm	Cho- les- terol mg	Car- bohy- drate gm
115.	Corn chips	1 oz.	28	155	2.0	9	1.8	0	16
116.	Cornflakes	1 c	25	97	2.0	0	0.0	0	21
117.	Cornmeal, degermed, yellow, enriched cooked	1/2 c	120	60	1.3	0	0.0	0	13
118.	Crackers, graham	2 squares	14	55	1.1	1	0.3	0	10
119.	Crackers, Ritz	1	3	15	0.2	1	0.2	0	2
120.	Crackers, saltines	4 squares	11	48	1.0	1	0.3	0	8
121.	Crackers, Soda	1	3	13	0.3	0	0.1	0	2
122.	Crackers, Triscuits	1	5	23	0.4	1	0.3	0	3
123.	Crackers, Wheat Thins	1	2	9	0.2	0	0.1	0	1
124.	Cream, light coffee or table	1 tbsp	15	20	0.5	2	0.5	5	1
125.	Cream, heavy whipping	1 tbsp	15	53	0.3	6	1.3	12	1
126.	Croissant	1	57	235	4.7	12	4.0	13	27
127.	Croissants (Sara Lee)	1 roll	18	59	1.6	2	0.3	0	8
128.	Cucumbers, raw pared	9 sm slices	28	4	0.3	0	0.0	0	1
129.	Dates hydrated	5	46	110	0.9	0	0.0	0	29
130.	Doughnuts, plain	1	42	164	1.9	8	2.0	19	22
131.	Dressing, blue cheese	1 tbsp	15	77	0.7	8	1.9	4	1
132.	Dressing, French	1 tbsp	16	83	0.1	9	1.4	0	1
133.	Dressing, Italian	1 tbsp	15	69	0.1	9	1.3	0	2
134.	Dressing, ranch style	1 tbsp	15	54	0.4	6	0.9	6	1
135.	Eggs, hard cooked	1 large	50	72	6.0	5	1.8	250	1
136.	Egg, fried with butter	1	46	95	5.4	6	2.4	278	1
137.	Egg McMuffin	1	138	327	18.5	15	5.9	259	31
138.	Egg salad sandwich	1	111	325	10.0	19	3.9	215	28
139.	Eggs, White	1 large	33	17	3.6	0	0.0	0	0
140.	Enchilada, beef	1	200	487	21.8	23	8.8	63	26
141.	Enchilada, cheese	1	230	632	25.3	34	17.6	82	31
142.	Farina, enriched, quick cooking, cooked	1/2 c	123	51	1.6	0	0.0	0	11
143.	Figs, dried	1 large	21	60	1.0	0	0.0	0	15
144.	Filet of Fish, McDonald's	1	131	402	15.0	23	7.9	43	34
145.	Fish, sticks	2	56	140	12.0	6	1.6	52	8
146.	Flounder	3 oz.	85	171	25.5	7	1.0	60	0
147.	Flour, all purpose enriched	1 c	125	455	13.0	1	0.0	0	95
148.	Flour, whole wheat	1 c	120	400	16.0	2	0.0	0	85
149.	Frankfurters, cooked	1	57	176	7.0	16	5.6	45	1
150.	Frankfurter, turkey/cooked	1	45	102	6.4	8	2.7	39	1
151.	Fruit cocktail	1 c	245	91	1.0	0	0.0	0	24
152.	Ginger ale	12 oz.	366	113	0.0	0	0.0	0	29
153.	Granola, Nature Valley	1/2 c	57	252	5.8	10	7.0	0	38
154.	Grapefruit, raw white	1/2 med	301	56	1.0	0	0.0	0	15
155.	Grapefruit, juice unsweetened canned	1/2 c	124	50	0.6	0	0.0	0	12
156.	Grapes, raw seedless European	10 grapes	50	34	0.3	0	0.0	0	9
157.	Grape juice, unsweetened bottled	1/2 c	127	84	0.3	0	0.0	0	21
158.	Gravy, beef, homemade	1 tbsp	17	19	0.3	2	1.0	1	1
159.	Haddock, fried (dipped in egg, milk, bread crumbs)	3 oz.	85	141	17.0	5	1.0	54	5
160.	Halibut, broiled with butter or margarine	3 oz.	85	144	21.0	6	2.1	55	0

Code	Food	Amount	Weight gm	Calo-ries	Pro-tein gm	Fat gm	Sat. Fat gm	Cho-les-terol mg	Car-bohy-drate gm
161.	Ham (cured pork)	3 oz.	85	318	20.0	26	9.4	77	0
162.	Ham, lunch meat	1 slice	28	37	5.5	1	0.5	13	0.3
163.	Hamburger, Big Mac	1	204	581	25.1	36	12.0	85	40
164.	Hamburger, McDonald's	1	99	257	13.0	9	3.7	26	30
165.	Honey	1 tbsp	21	64	0.0	0	0.0	0	17
166.	Ice cream, vanilla	1/2 c	67	135	3.0	7	4.4	27	14
167.	Ice cream cone	1 small	115	185	4.3	5	2.2	24	30
168.	Ice cream cone, Dairy Queen	medium	142	230	6.0	7	4.6	15	35
169.	Ice cream, hot fudge sund.	1	164	357	7.0	11	5.4	27	58
170.	Ice milk, vanilla	1/2 c	61	100	3.0	3	1.8	13	15
171.	Inst. breakfast/whole milk	1 c	281	280	15.0	8	5.1	33	34
172.	Jams or preserves	1 tbsp	7	18	0.0	0	0.0	0	5
173.	Jelly	1 tbsp	18	49	0.0	0	0.0	0	13
174.	Kale, fresh cooked, drained	1/2 c	55	22	2.5	0	0.0	0	3
175.	Kool Aid, with sugar	1 c	240	100	0.0	0	0.0	0	25
176.	Lamb leg, roast, trimmed	3 oz.	85	237	22.0	16	7.3	60	0
177.	Lasagna, homemade	1 piece	220	357	23.6	18	8.3	50	27
178.	Lemon juice, fresh	1 tbsp	15	4	0.1	0	0.0	0	1
179.	Lemonade (concentrate)	12 oz.	340	137	0.2	0	0.1	0	36
180.	Lentils, cooked	1/2 c	100	106	8.0	0	0.0	0	19
181.	Lettuce, crisp head	1 c sm chunks	75	10	0.7	0	0.0	0	2
182.	Lettuce, cos or romaine	1 c chopped	55	10	0.7	0	0.0	0	2
183.	Liver, beef, fried	1 slice 3 oz.	85	195	22.0	9	2.5	345	5
184.	Liverwurst, fresh	1 slice 1 oz.	28	87	5.0	7	3.5	50	1
185.	Lobster	1 c	145	138	27.0	2	1.0	293	0
186.	Macaroni, enriched cooked	1/2 c	70	78	2.4	0	0.0	0	16
187.	Macaroni and cheese	1/2 c	100	215	8.2	11	4.0	21	20
188.	Maple syrup	3 tbsp.	60	150	0.0	0	0.0	0	39
189.	Margarine	1 tsp	5	34	0.0	4	0.7	2	0
190.	Matzo	1 piece	30	117	3.0	0	0.0	0	25
191.	Mayonnaise	1 tsp	5	36	0.0	4	0.7	3	0
192.	Milk, evaporated whole	1/2 c	126	172	9.0	10	5.8	40	13
193.	Milk, lowfat (2% fat)	1 c	246	145	10.0	5	3.1	5	15
194.	Milk shake, chocolate	1 (10 fluid oz.)	340	433	11.5	13	7.8	45	70
195.	Milk shake, strawberry	1 (10 fluid oz.)	340	383	11.4	10	6.0	37	64
196.	Milk shake, vanilla (McDonald's)	1	289	323	10.0	8	5.1	29	52
197.	Milk skim	1 c	245	88	9.0	0	0.3	5	12
198.	Milk, whole (3.5% fat)	1 c	244	159	9.0	9	5.1	34	12
199.	Molasses, medium	1 tbsp	20	50	0.0	0	0.0	0	13
200.	Muffin, blueberry	1	45	135	3.0	5	1.5	19	20
201.	Muffin, bran	1	45	125	3.0	6	1.4	24	19
202.	Muffin, cornmeal	1	45	145	3.0	5	1.5	23	21
203.	Muffin, English w/butter	1	63	186	5.0	5	2.3	15	30
204.	Mushrooms, fresh cultivated	1/2 c sliced	35	12	1.0	0	0.0	0	2
205.	Mustard greens, cooked drained	1/2 c	70	16	1.7	0	0.0	0	3
206.	Noodles, egg, enriched cooked	1/2 c	80	100	3.3	1	0.0	0	19
207.	Nuts, Brazil	1 oz. (6-8 nuts)	28	185	4.1	19	4.8	0	3
208.	Nuts, pecans	1 oz.	28	195	2.6	20	1.4	0	4
209.	Nuts, walnuts	1 oz. (14 halves)	28	185	4.2	18	1.0	0	5

Code	Food	Amount	Weight gm	Calo-ries	Pro-tein gm	Fat gm	Sat. Fat gm	Cho-les-terol mg	Car-bohy-drate gm
210.	Oatmeal, quick, cooked	1/2 c	120	66	2.4	1	0.2	0	12
211.	Oil, soybean	1 tsp.	5	44	0.0	5	2.0	0	0
212.	Okra, cooked drained	1/2 c	80	23	1.6	0	0.0	0	5
213.	Olives, black ripe	10 extra large	55	61	0.5	7	1.0	0	1
214.	Onions, mature cooked, drained	1/2 c sliced	105	31	1.3	0	0.0	0	7
215.	Onion rings, fried	3	30	122	1.6	8	2.3	0	11
216.	Onion rings (Brazier) Dairy Queen	1 serving	85	360	6.0	17	6.0	15	33
217.	Orange, raw (medium skin)	1 med	180	64	1.3	0	0.0	0	16
218.	Orange juice, froz. reconstituted	1/2 c	125	61	0.9	0	0.0	0	15
219.	Oysters, raw Eastern	1/2 c (6-9 med)	120	79	10.0	2	1.3	60	4
220.	Pancakes	1 6" diam x 1/2" thick	73	169	5.2	5	1.0	36	25
221.	Papaya, raw	1/2 med	227	60	0.9	0	0.0	0	15
222.	Parsnips, cooked	1 large 9" long	160	106	2.4	1	0.0	0	24
223.	Peaches, raw, peeled	1 2¾" diam.	175	58	0.9	0	0.0	0	15
224.	Peaches, canned, heavy syrup	1 half 2⅛ tbsp liq.	96	75	0.4	0	0.0	0	19
225.	Peanut butter	2 tbsp	32	188	8.0	16	1.0	0	6
226.	Peanut butter/jam sandwich	1	100	340	11.4	14	2.6	0	45
227.	Peanuts, roasted	1 oz.	28	166	7.0	14	1.0	0	5
228.	Pears, Bartlett, raw	1 pear	180	100	1.1	1	0.0	0	25
229.	Pears, canned, heavy syrup	1 half 2¼ tbsp liq.	103	78	0.2	0	0.0	0	20
230.	Peas, frozen, cooked drained	1/2 c	80	55	4.1	0	0.0	0	10
231.	Peas, early, canned, drained	1/2 c	85	75	4.0	0	0.0	0	14
232.	Peppers, sweet, raw	1 pepper 3/4" × 3" diam.	200	36	2.0	0	0.0	0	8
233.	Pickles, dill	1 large 4" long	135	15	0.9	0	0.0	0	3
234.	Pickles, sweet	1 large 3" long	35	51	0.2	0	0.0	0	13
235.	Pineapple, raw	1/2 c diced	78	41	0.3	0	0.0	0	11
236.	Pineapple, canned, heavy syrup	1/2 c	128	95	0.4	0	0.0	0	25
237.	Pizza, Cheese, Thin 'n Crispy, Pizza Hut	1/2 10" pie	*	450	25.0	15	7.0	125	54
238.	Pizza, Cheese, Thick 'n Chewy, Pizza Hut	1/2 10" pie	*	560	34.0	14	6.0	110	71
239.	Plums, Japanese and hybrid, raw	1 plum 2⅛" diam.	70	32	0.3	0	0.0	0	8
240.	Popcorn, cooked/oil	1 c	11	55	0.9	3	0.5	0	6
241.	Popcorn, popped, plain, large kernel	1 c	6	12	0.8	0	0.0	0	5
242.	Pork, roast, trimmed	2 slices 3 oz.	85	179	24.0	8	2.2	65	0
243.	Pork, sausage, cooked	1 sm link	17	72	2.8	6	2.1	13	1
244.	Potato, baked in skin	1 potato 2⅓ × 4¼"	202	145	4.0	0	0.0	0	33
245.	Potato chips	10 chips	20	114	1.1	8	2.1	0	10
246.	Potato, French fried long	10 strips 3½–4"	78	214	3.4	10	1.7	0	28
247.	Potato, mashed, milk added	1/2 c	105	69	2.2	1	0.4	8	14
248.	Potato salad w/eggs/mayo	1/2 c	125	179	3.4	10	7.8	85	14
249.	Potatoes, hash brown	1/2 c	78	170	2.5	9	3.5	0	22
250.	Pound cake	1 piece	30	120	2.0	5	1.0	32	15
251.	Pretzel, thin, twists	1 oz.	28	113	2.8	1	0.3	0	23

Code	Food	Amount	Weight gm	Calories	Protein gm	Fat gm	Sat. Fat gm	Cholesterol mg	Carbohydrate gm
252.	Prunes, dried "softenized" without pits	5 prunes	61	137	1.1	0	0.0	0	36
253.	Prune juice, canned or bottled	1/2 c	128	99	0.5	0	0.0	0	24
254.	Pumpkin Pie	1 (3½")	114	241	4.6	13	3.0	70	28
255.	Quiche, Lorraine	1 piece	242	825	18.0	66	31.9	392	40
256.	Raisins, unbleached, seedless	1 oz.	28	82	0.7	0	0.0	0	22
257.	Rice, brown, cooked	1/2 c	96	116	2.5	1	0.0	0	25
258.	Rice Crispies (Kellogg's)	3/4 c	22	85	1.4	0	0.0	0	19
259.	Rice, white enriched, cooked	1/2 c	103	113	2.1	0	0.0	0	25
260.	Rueben sandwich	1	237	488	28.7	28	10.4	85	30
261.	Salami, dry	1 oz.	28	128	7.0	11	1.6	24	0
262.	Salmon, broiled with butter or margarine	3 oz.	85	156	23.0	6	2.2	53	0
263.	Salmon, canned Chinook	3 oz.	85	179	16.6	12	0.8	30	0
264.	Sardines, canned drained	1 oz.	28	58	7.0	3	1.0	20	0
265.	Sauerkraut, canned	1/2 c	118	21	1.2	0	0.0	0	5
266.	Sherbet	1/2 c	97	135	1.1	2	1.3	7	29
267.	Shredded Wheat-large bisc.	1	19	65	2.1	0	0.0	0	11
268.	Shrimp, boiled	3 oz.	85	99	18.0	1	0.1	128	1
269.	Soda pop, diet	12 oz.	340	2	0.0	0	0.0	0	0
270.	Soup, chicken, cream	1 c	248	191	7.5	12	4.6	27	15
271.	Soup, chicken noodle	1 c	241	75	4.0	2	0.7	7	9
272.	Soup, cream of mushroom condensed, prepared with equal volume of milk	1 c	245	216	7.0	14	5.4	15	16
273.	Soup, split pea, condensed, prepared with equal volume of water	1 c	245	145	9.0	3	1.1	0	21
274.	Soup, tomato, condensed, prepared with equal volume of water	1 c	245	88	2.0	3	0.5	0	16
275.	Soup, tomato with milk	1 c	248	160	6.0	6	2.9	17	22
276.	Soup, vegetable beef, condensed, prepared with equal volume of water	1 c	245	78	5.0	2	0.0	0	10
277.	Sour cream	1/2 c	115	247	3.6	24	16.3	51	5
278.	Spaghetti, in tomato sauce with cheese	1 c	250	260	8.8	9	2.0	10	37
279.	Spaghetti, with meatballs and tomato sauce	1 c	248	332	18.6	11.7	3.0	75	39
280.	Spareribs, cooked	3 oz.	85	377	17.8	33	12.0	73	0
281.	Spinach, raw, chopped	1 c	55	14	1.8	0	0.0	0	2
282.	Spinach, canned, drained	1/2 c	103	25	2.3	1	0.0	0	4
283.	Spinach, froz., cooked, drained	1/2 c	103	24	3.1	0	0.0	0	4
284.	Squash, summer, cooked	1/2 c	90	13	0.8	0	0.0	0	3
285.	Squash, winter, baked mashed	1/2 c	103	70	1.9	0	0.0	0	18
286.	Strawberries, raw	1 c	149	55	1.0	1	0.0	0	13
287.	Stuffing, bread, prepared	1/2 c	70	250	4.6	15	3.1	0	25
288.	Sundae, choc. Dairy Queen	medium	184	300	6.0	7	4.9	79	53
289.	Sugar, brown granulated	1 tsp	5	17	0.0	0	0.0	0	5
290.	Sugar, white granulated	1 tsp	4	15	0.0	0	0.0	0	4

Code	Food	Amount	Weight gm	Calo- ries	Pro- tein gm	Fat gm	Sat. Fat gm	Cho- les- terol mg	Car- bohy- drate gm
291.	Sweet potato, baked	1 potato 5" long	146	161	2.4	1	0.0	0	37
292.	Syrup (maple)	1 tbsp	20	50	0.0	0	0.0	0	13
293.	Taco, Taco Bell	1	83	186	15.0	8	0.0	0	14
294.	Tangerine	1 med 2⅜" diam.	116	39	0.7	0	0.0	0	10
295.	Tea, brewed	1/4 c	180	0	0.0	0	0.0	0	0
296.	Tomato juice, canned	1 c	244	42	1.9	0	0.1	0	10
297.	Tomato sauce (catsup)	1 tbsp	15	16	0.3	0	0.0	0	4
298.	Tomatoes, raw	1 tomato 3½ oz.	100	20	1.0	0	0.0	0	4
299.	Tomatoes, canned	1/2 c	121	26	1.2	0	0.0	0	5
300.	Tortilla chips	1 oz.	28	139	2.2	8	1.1	0	17
301.	Tortillas, corn, lime	1 6" diam.	30	63	1.5	1	0.0	0	14
302.	Tortilla, flour	1	35	105	2.6	3	0.4	0	19
303.	Tostada	1	148	200	9.2	8	3.0	14	25
304.	Tuna, canned, oil pack, drained	3 oz.	85	167	25.0	7	1.7	60	0
305.	Tuna, canned, water pack, solids and liquid	3½ oz.	99	126	27.7	1	0.0	55	0
306.	Turkey, roast (light and dark mixed)	3 oz.	85	162	27.0	5	1.5	73	0
307.	Turnip, cooked, drained	1/2 c cubed	78	18	0.6	0	0.0	0	4
308.	Turnip greens, cooked drained	1/2 c	73	19	2.1	0	0.0	0	3
309.	Veal, cooked loin	3 oz.	85	199	22.0	11	4.0	90	0
310.	Vegetables, mixed, cooked	1 c	182	116	5.8	0	0.0	0	24
311.	Watermelon	1 c diced	160	42	0.8	0	0.0	0	10
312.	Wheat germ, plain toasted	1 tbsp	6	23	1.8	1	0.0	0	3
313.	Whiskey, gin, rum, vodka 90 proof	1/2 11 oz (jigger)	42	110	0	0	0.0	0	0
314.	White cake, choc. icing	1 piece	71	268	3.5	11	3.7	2	40
315.	Whole wheat cereal, cooked	1/2 c	123	55	2.2	0	0.0	0	12
316.	Whole wheat flakes, ready-to-eat	1 c	30	106	3.1	1	0.0	0	24
317.	Whopper, Burger King	1	•	606	29.0	32	10.5	100	51
318.	Wine, dry table 12% alc.	3½ fl. oz.	102	87	0.1	0	0.0	0	4
319.	Wine, red dry 18.8% alc.	2 fl. oz.	59	81	0.1	0	0.0	0	5
320.	Yeast, brewers	1 tbsp	8	23	3.1	0	0.0	0	3
321.	Yogurt, fruit	1 c	227	231	9.9	2	1.6	10	43
322.	Yogurt, plain low fat	1 8-oz. container	226	113	7.7	4	2.3	15	12

Healthstyle: A Self-Test*

All of us want good health. But many of us do not know how to be as healthy as possible. Health experts now describe *lifestyle* as one of the most important factors affecting health. In fact, it is estimated that as many as seven of the ten leading causes of death could be reduced through common-sense changes in lifestyle. That's what this brief test, developed by the Public Health Service, is all about. Its purpose is simply to tell you how well you are doing to stay healthy. The behaviors covered in the test are recommended for most Americans. Some of them may not apply to persons with certain chronic diseases or handicaps, or to pregnant women. Such persons may require special instructions from their physicians.

10|18
12|9|92

Cigarette Smoking

If you *never smoke*, enter a score of 10 for this section and go to the next section on *Alcohol and Drugs*.

	Almost Always	Sometimes	Almost Never
1. I avoid smoking cigarettes.	2	1	0
2. I smoke only low tar and nicotine cigarettes *or* I smoke a pipe or cigars.	2	1	0

Smoking Score: _____10_____

---

* Source: National Health Information Clearinghouse. Washington, D.C.

Alcohol and Drugs

	Almost Always	Sometimes	Almost Never

1. I avoid drinking alcoholic beverages *or* I drink no more than 1 or 2 drinks a day.   **(4)** **(1)** 0

2. I avoid using alcohol or other drugs (especially illegal drugs) as a way of handling stressful situations or the problems in my life.   **(2)** 1 0

3. I am careful not to drink alcohol when taking certain medicines (for example, medicine for sleeping, pain, colds, and allergies), or when pregnant.   **(2)** 1 0

4. I read and follow the label directions when using prescribed and over-the-counter drugs.   **(2)** 1 0

Alcohol and Drugs Score: _____ 7

Eating Habits

	Almost Always	Sometimes	Almost Never

1. I eat a variety of foods each day, such as fruits and vegetables, whole grain breads and cereals, lean meats, dairy products, dry peas and beans, and nuts and seeds.   **(4)** **(1)** 0

2. I limit the amount of fat, saturated fat, and cholesterol I eat (including fat on meats, eggs, butter, cream, shortenings, and organ meats such as liver).   **(2)** 1 0

3. I limit the amount of salt I eat by cooking with only small amounts, not adding salt at the table, and avoiding salty snacks.   **(2)** 1 0

4. I avoid eating too much sugar (especially frequent snacks of sticky candy or soft drinks).   2 **(1)** 0

Eating Habits Score: _____ 6

Exercise/Fitness

	Almost Always	Sometimes	Almost Never

1. I maintain a desired weight, avoiding overweight and underweight. — **3** 1 0

2. I do vigorous exercises for 15–30 minutes at least 3 times a week (examples include running, swimming, brisk walking). — **3** 1 0

3. I do exercises that enhance my muscle tone for 15–30 minutes at least 3 times a week (examples include yoga and calisthenics). — **2** **1** 0

4. I use part of my leisure time participating in individual, family, or team activities that increase my level of fitness (such as gardening, bowling, golf, and baseball). — 2 **1** 0

Exercise/Fitness Score: ___9___

Stress Control

	Almost Always	Sometimes	Almost Never

1. I have a job or do other work that I enjoy. — **2** 1 0

2. I find it easy to relax and express my feelings freely. — 2 **1** 0

3. I recognize early, and prepare for, events or situations likely to be stressful for me. — 2 **1** 0

4. I have close friends, relatives, or others whom I can talk to about personal matters and call on for help when needed. — **2** 1 0

5. I participate in group activities (such as church and community organizations) or hobbies that I enjoy. — **2** 1 0

Stress Control Score: ___9___

Safety

1. I wear a seat belt while riding in a car.   ②   1   0

2. I avoid driving while under the influence of alcohol and other drugs.   2 ① 0

3. I obey traffic rules and the speed limit when driving.   2 ① 0

4. I am careful when using potentially harmful products or substances (such as household cleaners, poisons, and electrical devices).   ② 1 0

5. I avoid smoking in bed.   ② 1 0

Safety Score:

What Your Scores Mean to YOU

Scores of 9 and 10

Excellent! Your answers show that you are aware of the importance of this area to your health. More important, you are putting your knowledge to work for you by practicing good health habits. As long as you continue to do so, this area should not pose a serious health risk. It's likely that you are setting an example for your family and friends to follow. Since you got a very high test score on this part of the test, you may want to consider other areas where your scores indicate room for improvement.

Scores of 6 to 8

Your health practices in this area are good, but there is room for improvement. Look again at the items you answered with a "Sometimes" or "Almost Never." What changes can you make to improve your score? Even a small change can often help you achieve better health.

Scores of 3 to 5

Your health risks are showing! Would you like more information about the risks you are facing and about why it is important for you to change these behaviors? Perhaps you need help in deciding how to successfully make the changes you desire. In either case, help is available.

Scores of 0 to 2

Obviously, you were concerned enough about your health to take the test, but your answers show that you may be taking serious and unnecessary risks with your health. Perhaps you are not aware of the risks and what to do about them. You can easily get the information and help you need to improve, if you wish. The next step is up to you.

YOU Can Start Right Now!

In the test you just completed were numerous suggestions to help you reduce your risk of disease and premature death. Here are some of the most significant:

 Avoid cigarettes. Cigarette smoking is the single most important preventable cause of illness and early death. It is especially risky for pregnant women and their unborn babies. Persons who stop smoking reduce their risk of getting heart disease and cancer. So if you're a cigarette smoker, think twice about lighting that next cigarette. If you choose to continue smoking, try decreasing the number of cigarettes you smoke and switching to a low tar and nicotine brand.

 Follow sensible drinking habits. Alcohol produces changes in mood and behavior. Most people who drink are able to control their intake of alcohol and to avoid undesired, and often harmful, effects. Heavy, regular use of alcohol can lead to cirrhosis of the liver, a leading cause of death. Also, statistics clearly show that mixing drinking and driving is often the cause of fatal or crippling accidents. So if you drink, do it wisely and in moderation. ***Use care in taking drugs.*** Today's greater use of drugs — both legal and illegal — is one of our most serious health risks. Even some drugs prescribed by your doctor can be dangerous if taken when drinking alcohol or before driving. Excessive or continued use of tranquilizers (or "pep pills") can cause physical and mental problems. Using or experimenting with illicit drugs such as marijuana, heroin, cocaine, and PCP may lead to a number of damaging effects or even death.

Eat sensibly. Overweight individuals are at greater risk for diabetes, gall bladder disease, and high blood pressure. So it makes good sense to maintain proper weight. But good eating habits also mean holding down the amount of fat (especially saturated fat), cholesterol, sugar and salt in your diet. If you must snack, try nibbling on fresh fruits and vegetables. You'll feel better — and look better, too.

Exercise regularly. Almost everyone can benefit from exercise — and there's some form of exercise almost everyone can do. (If you have any doubt, check first with your doctor.) Usually, as little as 15–30 minutes of vigorous exercise three times a week will help you have a healthier heart, eliminate excess weight, tone up sagging muscles, and sleep better. Think how much difference all these improvements could make in the way you feel!

Learn to handle stress. Stress is a normal part of living; everyone faces it to some degree. The causes of stress can be good or bad, desirable or undesirable (such as a promotion on the job or the loss of a spouse). Properly handled, stress need not be a problem. But unhealthy responses to stress — such as driving too fast or erratically, drinking too much, or prolonged anger or grief — can cause a variety of physical and mental problems. Even on a very busy day, find a few minutes to slow down and relax. Talking over a problem with someone you trust can often help you find a satisfactory solution. Learn to distinguish between things that are "worth fighting about" and things less important.

Be safety conscious. Think "safety first" at home, at work, at school, at play, and on the highway. Buckle seat belts and obey traffic rules. Keep poisons and weapons out of the reach of children, and keep emergency numbers by your telephone. When the unexpected happens, you'll be prepared.

Where Do You Go From Here:

Start by asking yourself a few frank questions: *Am I really doing all I can to be as healthy as possible? What steps can I take to feel better? Am I willing to begin now?* If you scored low in one or more *sections* of the test, decide what changes you want to make for improvement. You might pick that aspect of your lifestyle where you feel you have the best chance for success and tackle that one first. Once you have improved your score there, go on to other areas.

If you already have tried to change your health habits (to stop smoking or exercise regularly, for example), don't be discouraged if you haven't yet succeeded. The difficulty you have encountered may be due to influences you've never really thought about — such as advertising — or to a lack of support and encouragement. Understanding these influences is an important step toward changing the way they affect you.

There's Help Available. In addition to personal actions you can take on your own, there are community programs and groups (such as the YMCA or the local chapter of the American Heart Association) that can assist you and your family to make the changes you want to make. If you want to know more about these groups or about health risks, contact your local health department or the National Health Information Clearinghouse. There's a lot you can do to stay healthy or to improve your health — and there are organizations that can help you. Start a new HEALTHSTYLE today!

Index

*Calcium - 1000-1200 mg.
Sodium - 1200 mg (same or < cal.)
cholestorol - 250mg
Fat - 40gms
cals/day - 1200 mininum

Carbo -
Fat - 30%
Protein -